SAVING
THE SAVING GOSPEL

STEVE WEST

SAVING THE SAVING GOSPEL

STEVE WEST

5317 Wye Creek Dr, Frederick, MD 21703-6938
Website: newcovenantmedia.com
Email: info@newcovenantmedia.com
Phone: 301-473-8781 or 800-376-4146
Fax: 240-206-0373

Saving the Saving Gospel

Copyright 2008© by Steve West

Published by: New Covenant Media
5317 Wye Creek Drive
Frederick, Maryland 21703-6938

Orders: www.newcovenantmedia.com

All rights reserved. No part of this publication may be reproduced, stored in a retrieval system, or transmitted in any form by any means, electronic, mechanical, photocopy, recording, or otherwise without the prior permission of the publisher, except as provided by USA copyright law.

Printed in the United States of America

ISBN 13: 978-1-928965-26-8

All Scripture quotations are from the HOLY BIBLE, NEW INTERNATIONAL VERSION®. Copyright © 1973, 1978, 1984 International Bible Society. Used by permission of Zondervan. All rights reserved.

Acknowledgements

I would like to thank Madoc Baptist Church for their continued spiritual fellowship and patience. Mike Sanderson provided me with several opportunities to teach the material in the first part of this book to camp staffs across Canada. Mike has been a great partner in ministry and a great friend in life. Heather Roundsky has been more enthusiastic about my work than I am, and has encouraged me tremendously. Thanks so much.

I dedicate this book to my wife Heather. Our two daughters, Charlotte and Brooklyn, are blessed to have Heather not only as their mother, but as a mother who has been wise enough to realize that no amount of money or career advancement is more valuable than raising her young children. Heather, Charlotte, and Brooklyn are continual reminders of God's abundant grace. Besides the Lord Jesus Christ, my family is the richest treasure I have. I love you.

Table of Contents

Introduction *1*
Chapter One–The God Who Is *7*
Chapter Two–More About The God Who Is *21*
Chapter Three–The Fall Into Sin *35*
Chapter Four–Salvation in Jesus Christ *45*
Chapter Five–A Saving Salvation *57*
Chapter Six–Surveying Reality *69*
Chapter Seven–God's Created Order *79*
Chapter Eight–The Evil in the Order *91*
Chapter Nine–The Resurrection *105*
Chapter Ten–Epistemology *119*
Chapter Eleven–Conclusion *131*

Introduction

At one level the title of this book is odd, if not odious. The gospel saves *us*; we do not save the gospel. How can the saving gospel be in need of saving? On the other hand, any variety of non-Christian readers may be offended by the connotation that the gospel is in fact something that *is* saving. Of course the gospel needs saving—it is an antiquated, politically incorrect embarrassment. From this perspective the gospel needs to be saved from itself. It cannot save, and so if it is to be preserved at all, it must be saved by sophisticated thinkers living in a technologically advanced age who have no difficulty with editing ancient texts. Better yet, just consign it to the rubbish bin or to the shelf next to the books of Greek mythology. For others, like a select number of religious professors, the saving of the gospel is not to be attempted by either its exclusive acceptance (*pace* evangelical Christianity) or its outright rejection (*pace* militant atheists). In this model the gospel can be honored as something which does in fact bring salvation, provided the Christian understands that other religions or faiths are just as sufficient for bringing salvation to their adherents. Yes, the gospel saves, but no more so than sincerely following Islam.

To clear up any confusion, let me explain a little bit about what I intended by entitling this book *Saving the Saving Gospel*. First, and above everything else, I believe that the gospel of Jesus Christ is truly a gospel that saves. I do not believe that the gospel is one among many saving options scattered throughout the world of religious beliefs and practices. The gospel alone is saving. It is in the very nature and essence of the gospel that it alone deals with the world's real problem (sin) by providing a genuine solution (atonement) through a perfect person (Jesus Christ). Unless sin is properly identified as the problem—and sin can only be properly identified after the character of God is properly identified—any number of solutions may seem plausible. Yet part of the problem is that we think we are competent to perform a self-diagnosis, and then to prescribe ourselves the necessary dosage of beliefs and practices to save ourselves. On the contrary, we need to have our disease named for us, and the disease is called sin.

When we speak of the saving gospel it is assumed that we are being saved *from* something. If I was vacationing at an all-inclusive beach resort on the ocean (which sounds awfully nice sitting here after the longest Canadian winter I've ever experienced) and a boat pulled up on shore to "rescue" me, I would be disinclined to get aboard. There would be nothing they were saving me from. If, on the other hand, a riptide pulled me out into the ocean and a boat pulled up alongside me offering assistance, I would gladly take it. The difference, of course, is that in the first situation I am not in danger and in the second I am. In the gospel, we find out that we require salvation from sin, death, and hell. We also require salvation from God. As paradoxical as it sounds, God saves us from ourselves and from himself. He saves us *from* himself by saving us *for* himself, and he does this *by* himself.

Secondly, the title of this book reveals that I think there is some way in which the saving gospel does stand in need of saving. Saving the gospel does not mean correcting its deficiencies (for it has no deficiencies to correct), nor does it mean that the gospel is weak and desperately in need of our mighty assistance. In reality, saving the gospel largely means nothing more than leaving it as fully intact as possible. It means unmasking false claimants who change the Bible's theology but who still insist on referring to their new creation as the gospel. It means studying the gospel and being mastered by it. It means learning the message of the Scriptures, and passing it on as clearly and as accurately as possible. It means that we obey and "contend for the faith that was once for all entrusted to the saints," (Jude 3b).

Lastly, saving the saving gospel can be illustrated not only in the Scriptures, but down through the centuries of church history. Paul the apostle labored to save the saving gospel from its opponents (read Galatians—he labored with verve!). John fought against something like proto-Gnosticism. The next few centuries after the apostolic age saw the church faithfully wage battles against Arianism and Nestorianism, not to mention other heresies. Church councils were convened for the express purpose of saving the saving gospel. Fast forwarding a millennium of history (as Protestants are in the terrible habit of doing) we arrive at the Reformation. Martin Luther discovered that the saving gospel of Jesus Christ had been dreadfully perverted. So he went to work, doing his utmost to save the saving gospel from the corrupt and ignorant hands into which its message had fallen. We will have to forgo detailing others such as John Hus or John Bunyan, who respectively endured martyrdom and incarceration for the freedom of the gospel. We will also pause here and allow later generations to retrospectively identify the heroes of our contemporaries who labor to save the saving gospel. I have my opinions about some individuals and groups who are working in this vein today, but I will not indulge myself in either their praise or criticism. Suffice it to say that God's people have endeavored to save the saving gospel from the time of the apostles down to the present, and that such work is both necessary and vital. We owe future generations this work of saving the saving gospel, because past generations faithfully, and at great cost, saved it for us by the grace of God.

Saving the saving gospel is also a debt we owe if we have in fact been saved. It is a duty laid upon every believer. For the glory of God and the Lord Jesus Christ, we dare not let the gospel be lost on our watch. What does it say about us as followers of Christ if we are unconcerned with the message of the gospel? All around, people perish, and all around, false witnesses go door to door with a dangerous false gospel on their lips. All around, churches subtly change the truth and Satan sits in the choir loft like an angel of light. All around, theologians deconstruct the Bible, and edit the Bible, and reject the Bible. All around, ostensibly evangelical Christians sit back "saved," waiting for the Second Coming or primetime TV, whichever comes first. Salvation apparently means nothing more to many professing Christians than that they get to live in a fashion identical to the world around them, but then when they die they get to go to heaven (which is just like the world but a little more colorful, a little nicer, a little cleaner, and a little more comfortable).

Like Luther, saving the saving gospel is going to take place in the confessing church first. It is only when believers can carry on a biblically informed conversation about soteriology (i.e., the doctrine of salvation) that they will be ready to carry on an evangelistic and apologetic conversation with someone outside of the church. Apologetics is the field of study and thinking that seeks to defend the faith. Clearly if one is wishing to defend the faith one needs to understand what the faith is in the first place. Apologetics is not primarily bound up with quoting a handful of statistics about the mathematical improbabilities of evolution. We are at risk of creating a fear-mongering group of evangelicals who can fight about evolution but who can't explain *why* Jesus' death on the cross is necessary for salvation. They can tell you that in order to be saved you need to believe that Jesus died on the cross and then ask him into your heart—but they can't explain what that means, for the simple reason that everything they know about the gospel is contained in that utterly insufficient cliché. "What's that? You want to know why you need to believe in Jesus' death on the cross in order to be saved from your sins? That's a good question. Let's come back to it, if we have time, but first let's discuss why Darwin was probably wrong."

Classically expressed, the position of this book is in broad sympathy with the school of thought that sees "faith seeking understanding." It is the biblical gospel that saves, and biblical and theological truths need to be understood in order for the gospel to be saved from distortion. Apologetic arguments are secondary, and should be derived from the gospel itself. In other words, apologetic arguments must not be detached and isolated from the faith that is being defended. Defending the faith assumes there is a faith that is being defended. The objective faith is logically prior to its own defense.

With such a background understanding tucked away in our minds, we will now proceed to examine the biblical message of the saving gospel. The first four chapters of this book will attempt to trace out the flow and logic of the gospel. The remaining chapters will examine some of the arguments that are currently used by apologists in the defense of the faith. Let me be perfectly clear: This book only "saves" the gospel to the extent that it accurately articulates the saving gospel of Jesus Christ. Furthermore, I envision the purpose of this book to be less about polemics than positive theological construction. Although there is a place for even-handed yet rigorous assessments of things like modern ecumenical movements, the new perspective on Pauline justification, etc., my concern is more pastoral. I am purposefully trading nuances on the borders for solid foundations in the center. Still, like all honest communicators, I hope that the finished work is fair, accurate, and helpful. Naturally, I also hope that the subject matter is not oversimplified to the point of distortion. What follows, then, is little more than an attempt to look at the biblical message of salvation in such a way as to "keep the main thing the main thing."

Chapter One

THE GOD WHO IS

There are so many competing definitions and views of the nature and character of God that one is almost driven to despair. What hope, if any, exists for truly understanding God? While we may derive some comfort from saying: "I feel God is like such and such," or "It seems to me God is probably like this or that," it should be clear that my opinion of God does not for one moment have any bearing on what God is actually like. An opinion is false if it is not in conformity to fact, or if it does not correspond to the way things really are. Simply saying something does not make it true.

For example, I can say that God is too nice to punish people for the wicked things that they have done. I can say that, and I can even believe it, but that does not make it true, for the rather obvious reason that I could be completely mistaken. In fact, if we are being ruthlessly honest, most of what is said about God is pure guesswork with no rationale behind it at all. Subjective hunches rule the field, and since one subjective opinion is as good as another, in the end all hunches are given equal standing. Well, at least the nice hunches about a kind God are all permitted.

Thankfully, this grim situation can be easily remedied. God is not an abstract concept to be colored any way we wish. God is an objective being, and he has revealed himself to human beings. This revelation has not taken the form of veiled hints and subtle clues, as if God has provided us with a riddle based map to buried treasure. No, God's revelation is exceptionally clear. He has, as a matter of fact, actually *spoken*. He has given us a verbal, written revelation. If we want to know who God is and what he is like, we must avail ourselves of his actual words. Instead of us *guessing* that God is like *x*, God has *told* us that he is like *y*. Presumably God knows himself a little better than we do, and so we would be more than a tiny bit foolish to reject his self-revelation to preserve our own guesses or feelings. What we think about God must be derived from, and line up with, God's own gracious self-disclosure in the Scriptures.

In the following pages we will attempt to examine some of the riches of the nature and character of God. These characteristics, or attributes, are not exhaustive, nor do we understand them with perfect comprehension. There is a depth to God that we cannot plumb. God can be truly known by human beings, but he cannot be exhaustively comprehended. Only an infinite being can understand and know everything about an infinite being. Only God can fully comprehend himself, but he has made humans in his image so that we can understand him well enough to say we truly know him.

It is now time to turn our attention to some of the particular attributes of God. Again, let it be clearly understood that the saving message of the gospel does not function in a vacuum. The gospel only makes sense to an individual who has a basic understanding of the real character of God.

1. Self-Existent

The Bible begins in the beginning (Gen. 1:1). Since God inspired the Bible correctly, this fact must be significant.

God does not start his revelation of himself in the Scriptures with a pitch about asking his son Jesus into your heart. He begins with himself. He is just there, existing. Before the origins of time and the universe God is existent. In the beginning nothing can create God because nothing other than God exists. God creates the heavens and the earth (which is a merism for "everything"). Life does not emerge blindly out of a non-sentient, impersonal, and amoral universe; the universe emerges from one who is living, intelligent, personal, and moral.

God brings order and life into existence by speaking. "God said" is the refrain at the start of each creative day, and throughout each day God "called" and "said" and "blessed" repeatedly. The God who exists is a God who speaks. He is not a waster of words, nor are his words ineffectual or impotent. To bring a universe into existence, God just has to say the word. To bring together a rich diversity in an underlying unity God merely needs to speak. For him, to will is to achieve. God's will, represented by his speech, accomplishes its purpose. Perhaps the first lesson God wants us to learn is that he exists, and that his word is powerful enough to bring a very good universe into existence. Remember this point, because it is integral to a proper understanding of the gospel. Much more will be said about this truth later.

God's self-existence is also called his aseity. Aseity can be expressed in a negative way (i.e., God does not depend on anything else for his existence) and in a positive way (i.e., God exists in himself because it is in his very nature or essence to exist). Nothing else that exists has this characteristic. Everything else that exists is dependent on the existence of God.

Not only is this doctrine important to establish at the outset, but it also appears at a most critical moment of God's self-revelation to the nation of Israel. When God manifests himself to Moses in the burning bush, he reveals his name (i.e., the essence of his nature) as: "I AM WHO I AM," (Ex. 3:14). God just is who he is. God is the LORD. The LORD is God. His identity and existence are fully self-contained. He is independent, self-sufficient, and self-existent. God knows the significance of his own name—he knows all that he is. The nature of deity is coextensive with the necessary existence and character of YHWH. Who is God? He is the God Who Is.

2. Eternal

Philosophers love to debate about the existence and meaning of time. Such discussions, stimulating as they may be, will be bypassed here. All that needs to be noted is that human beings are temporally bounded creatures. We self-consciously perceive our existence in an ordered sequence of moments. Armchair philosophy aside, we divide our lives into the three spheres of past, present, and future. Our whole lives take place in this passing stream of time. What I once thought of as tomorrow becomes today and passes into yesterday, with another tomorrow taking its place and setting up the chain all over again.

The eternality of God, at its most basic level, means that there was never a "time" when God did not exist. That God always has been, and always will be, is the most important point. He did not come into existence, nor will he ever cease to exist. Without being overly fussy on precise terminology, this idea can be generally expressed by saying that God always existed in eternity past, and will always exist in eternity future.

If we desire to be a little more accurate, however, we need to understand that a phrase like "eternity past" cannot be taken with an extreme literalism. Indeed, the space-*time* universe only began to exist when God created it. God is the creator of time in the same way that he is the creator of matter (God is spirit, not corporeal, so matter is something he created). Time and matter are created together in the same act. So if we conceive of "eternity past" as just a really, *really* long time, we are off track. (There is a mathematical argument against an actual infinite amount of time in the past that we will examine in a subsequent chapter.)

What exactly does it mean to exist before time? I confess I have a very hard time understanding this idea. I suspect we all do. This is not owing to the incoherency of the concept, however. On the contrary, it is owing to our finite, time-bound nature. Time is certainly not something that is "necessary" in any way. So, time can *not* exist, and this is not too difficult to understand. What it would be like to exist, however, before time (note how I am forced to use the chronological indicator "before" even though it does not really apply!) is something that I cannot articulate.

God is in some sense outside of the domain of time, but he does act *in* time. He knows what time it is. At the present, this means that God knows that it is 9:41 a.m. in my time zone as I type this sentence (presuming that the clock on my computer is accurate: if it is not, God knows the real time *and* he knows that my computer clock is inaccurate). Now, this is all quite remarkable, but not contradictory. It is just one area in which we who are so finite and limited cannot fully understand a personal being that transcends our experiences and concepts.

Moses noted the relationship between God's eternality and human temporality in a prayer which is recorded in Psalm 90. He prayed: "Lord, you have been our dwelling place throughout all generations. Before the mountains were born or you brought forth the earth and the world, from everlasting to everlasting you are God. You turn men back to dust, saying, 'Return to dust, O sons of men.' For a thousand years in your sight are like a day that has just gone by, or like a watch in the night," (v. 1-4). In contrast, human beings are like grass that withers (v. 5-6), with a seventy or eighty year life span (v. 10). If even one thousand years are like a watch in the night to God, what is our lifetime of seventy or eighty?

3. Omnipresent

Not only are we temporally limited, we are also spatially limited. Probably all of us have been in a dilemma about where to be at a given time, when there are two events we would like to attend that are taking place simultaneously at two different locations. We can attend either Charlotte's ballet recital or Brooklyn's volleyball game, but we cannot attend both since they are both occurring at 4 p.m. on the same Saturday in venues that are 50 miles apart. Being corporeal (i.e., having a body) means, amongst other things, to be spatially extended. My body takes up a mathematically defined amount of room. Since my size relative to the universe is quite small, I can only ever be at a small fraction of the places where I would like to be. Being somewhere is a limiting and exclusive position for me: being *here* for me only makes sense against the negative of *not* being *there* at the same time. I may be able to go to the place I designate as *there*, but then I have to leave the place I currently call *here*. Obviously, the only thing this means is that you can't be in two places at once!

God, in contrast to us, is not spatially extended, and furthermore he is not spatially limited. He is omnipresent, or everywhere. While I write this, my hands are on the keyboard of my computer, and my feet are flat on the floor. There is a sense in which I am everywhere that a part of my body is found, but there is another equally true sense in which even the parts of my body are not at the same place at the same time. My feet are somewhere other than where my hands are, and vice versa. God's omnipresence does not mean that he is just bigger than the universe ("He's got the whole wide world in his hands" is metaphorically, not spatially correct). God is not to be imagined as just larger than the universe or smaller than a subatomic particle. He is not everywhere in the sense of extending through all the far-flung reaches of space. His feet are not on Jupiter with his head sticking outside the borders of the known universe. Rather, God is everywhere in the sense of being fully and comprehensively present at every point of space. All of God is in every place.

This doctrine is classically expressed in the language of Psalm 139:7-10: "Where can I go from your Spirit? Where can I flee from your presence? If I go up to the heavens, you are there; if I make my bed in the depths, you are there. If I rise on the wings of the dawn, if I settle on the far side of the sea, even there your hand will guide me, your right hand will hold me fast." The psalmist David is not implying that God can beat him to wherever it is that he wants to go. It is not as if David can attempt to flee from God, only to discover that God has taken a short-cut and has arrived at the intended destination first. David cannot get away from God because God is *already* present in *every* physical location. God is no more absent from hell than he is from heaven. He is fully present in both heaven and hell, although he manifests himself differently in those locations. Hell is not marked by the absence of God—it is the place where guilty sinners are continually confronted with the God Who Is. Heaven, by way of contrast, is the place where redeemed sinners are continually confronted with the God Who Is. God's presence means either salvation or damnation for human beings. This is why when the Bible speaks of God "visiting" people it is either in terms of blessing or judgment.

4. Omnipotent

God is perfectly strong and possesses limitless strength. There is nothing that God cannot do, except for that which is outside of the logical and moral bounds of his character. For example, there is a very real sense in which God does not have the ability to lie. He does not have the power to cease to exist. Yet unless we want to become overly pedantic, it should be clear that this attribute functions in a positive way. God is never too weak to achieve his goals. He never runs into an opposing force which seriously challenges his strength. Whatever God desires to do, achieve, or accomplish, he has the ability to realize. I could exercise every day of my life and never be strong enough to play in the NFL. My actual power is limited, and my potential power is limited, too. God's power knows no bounds or limitations at all.

This morning I had the opportunity to be a guest teacher in our local high school's world religions course. I was the Christian "authority" thrown to the grade eleven lions. The students were actually remarkably attentive, polite, and engaged, and they asked very thoughtful questions. One girl asked how Christians deal with logical contradictions, like whether or not God is able to make a stone so big he can't lift it. There have been many different responses given to this objection against the coherency of God's omnipotence, but only one will be taken up here.

Perhaps the most stimulating discussion I have read on the "Paradox of the Stone" is the article by C. Wade Savage.[1] Without reproducing his whole line of argumentation, Savage notes that the question needs to be broken down into component parts. For the first part, the real question is: "Is God the perfect stone maker?" The answer to this question is "Yes." God can make any kind of stone, with any size, shape, or weight you would like. There is no stone that God cannot make. For the second part, the real question is: "Is God the perfect stone lifter?" The answer to this question, like the first, is "Yes." God can lift any stone, no matter what its size, shape, or weight.

God, then, is a perfect stone maker *and* a perfect stone lifter. These are two positive traits. God is omnipotent in his stone making, and omnipotent in his stone lifting. There are no limits on the stones he can make or on the stones he

---

[1] C. Wade Savage, "The Paradox of the Stone," *The Philosophical Review* 76, (1967) : 74-79

can lift. Now, the only way this paradox can succeed, then, is if "being the perfect stone maker" also involves "being able to make a stone that God cannot lift." But why should being the perfect stone maker entail such a thing? If there is no such thing as a stone that God cannot lift, how is it the stone maker's fault that he cannot make one? After all, the stone maker can make any stone of any size or weight! And it just so happens that the perfect stone lifter can lift any stone of any size or weight! God is both: his omnipotence is displayed in both his limitless stone making ability, and in his limitless stone lifting power. Mental riddles aside, God is utterly omnipotent, with no external limits at all.

5. Omniscient

God knows everything about everything (cf., I John 3:20). Think about that. He knows the number of cells in my left ring finger. He knows the number of atoms that comprise Saturn. He knows every word in every book in every language that has ever been written. God knows everything that took place in the past, and he knows everything that will take place in the future. God has never had to think through a difficult problem in an attempt to come up with a solution—there simply are no difficult problems for God in the first place. I read books because there are so many things I do not know or understand, and I need to learn. God never *learns*, because there is literally nothing that he does not already know.

As a corollary to this, God has never been wrong. Unlike my wife, I am forever getting facts, dates, and events confused. My memory can be quite inaccurate, and I make mistakes and errors in a variety of ways. "I didn't know that" is a phrase I find myself saying frequently. This is a phrase that God has *never* said; not because he's stubborn, but because it would be untrue.

6. Wise

Although it is not as common, the awesome wisdom of God is sometimes referenced by the term omnisapient (i.e., all-wise). Knowledge and wisdom are closely aligned, but they are not identical. The bare facts that constitute knowledge must be applied properly in order for the knower to be considered wise. Some people seem to know a great deal of theory, but they are not able to translate this theory into practice. For God, there is no such disjunction between his perfect knowledge and his perfect wisdom.

Wayne Grudem's definition of God's wisdom is right on the mark: "God's wisdom means that God always chooses the best goals and the best means to those goals."[2] Since God knows everything, there is no piece of data that he overlooks. From his exhaustive knowledge he sees every possible goal, and with his matchless wisdom he selects the very best goals, and the very best means to achieve them. God never realizes midstream that he is heading towards the wrong destination, or that he is taking the wrong path to where he wants to go. On the contrary, he always knows the best destination, and the best way to get there.

It has been commonly said that if you were as powerful as God you would probably make lots of changes to the universe, but if you were as wise as God you would not change a thing. God's ways—including God's timeframe—are perfect. The changes we perceive do not happen one

---

[2] Wayne Grudem, *Systematic Theology: An Introduction to Biblical Doctrine* (Grand Rapids: Zondervan, 1994), 193.

second sooner, or one second later, than a perfectly wise being allows. For human beings, the wisest thing we can do is submit to the greater wisdom of the omnisapient God. Thinking that God is truly mistaken about anything is not only morally reprehensible, it is utterly foolish.

7. Sovereign

The last attribute of God to be examined in this chapter is his sovereignty. More will be said about the relationship between God's sovereignty and the existence of evil and suffering later on. For now we will have to be content with setting forth the basic contour of the doctrine. When it comes to the sovereignty of God, there is certainly not a lack of biblical teaching on the subject! From Genesis to Revelation, God is the ruling, reigning, and sovereign king of the universe. Absolutely *everything* that happens in the universe—including the acts of human beings—is part of the plan of God who is working out all things in conformity to his will and eternal, wise purposes (cf., Eph. 1:11).

This general principle finds expression in many biblical particulars. John Reisinger has helpfully identified some of the areas in the Scriptures in which God is said to be in sovereign control. He notes the following:

I. God has a definite plan and purpose for the world. Job 23:13; Eph. 1:8-12.

II. God is always in control of all things and is constantly at work in accomplishing His plan. Hab. 1:1-11; Isa. 10:5, 6.

III. God controls and uses everyone, even the devil, in working out His plan. Isa. 10:7-11; Ps. 76:10.

IV. God punishes the people that He uses to accomplish His purposes when they act out of wrong motives. Isa. 10:12-16; Acts 2:23, 24; Mt. 27:15-26.

V. All things are from God, but the devil is the agent of all evil. II Sam. 24:1; I Chron. 21:1.

VI. Although all sickness and affliction are part of God's purposes and under His sovereign control, it does not follow that all sickness and affliction are necessarily chastisement for sin. Job 1:1, 6-2:10; 13:15.[3]

Much more biblical data could be adduced to buttress these statements. Some of these themes will be treated with more rigor in the section on the relationship between God's sovereignty and the existence of evil in the universe. Make no mistake: human beings are fully responsible for all that they do, but God is in sovereign control over everything that happens. Some fatalists have focused so much on God's sovereignty that they have lost human responsibility, while others have started with an erroneous definition of "freedom" which has resulted in a denial of God's comprehensive sovereignty. Both positions fail to do justice to the biblical data.

Summary

In this chapter we have taken a cursory look at the God Who Is. God is self-existent, eternal, omnipresent, omnipotent, omniscient, omnisapient, and sovereign. When you read over this list of attributes, it is not surprising that a being with these characteristics is sovereign! As awesome as these attributes are, they are also only part of the nature of

---

[3] John G. Reisinger, *The Sovereignty of God in Providence* (Frederick, MD: New Covenant Media, ND), 1.

God. In his grace, God has revealed far more about his character to us. We will now turn to consider this further revelation.

Chapter Two

MORE ABOUT THE GOD WHO IS

We can take comfort in the strength, knowledge, and sovereign rule of God because—and *only* because—he has a perfect moral nature. It would be unimaginably terrifying if we lived in a universe with an omnipotent being who was thoroughly evil. The God Who Is does not just have raw, unlimited power, or brute factual knowledge. God is a personal being, to whom the personal pronoun "he" is applied. He has a personality, a personal nature, and a moral character. God's revelation does not just consist in his telling us about his infinite capabilities (e.g., "Just so you know, there is no object I cannot lift, because my strength is unlimited."). No, God has revealed himself in a very intimate and personal way. His self-revelation is filled with glimpses into his mind, heart, and character. There are things God tells us he loves, and things he tells us he hates. There are things which bring him pleasure, and there are things of which he entirely disapproves. Some attitudes are acceptable to him, and others are not. Certain behaviors are honoring to him, and others are completely unacceptable and abhorrent. God is a discriminating moral being, who personally identifies the difference between what is right and what is wrong. Let us now begin to examine some of the personal characteristics of God that he has so graciously revealed.

1. Holy

More than two and a half millennia ago, Isaiah the prophet was given an incredible vision. He saw the Lord God seated on a throne, and angels were flying around him calling out: "Holy, holy, holy, is the Lord Almighty; the whole earth is full of his glory," (Isaiah 6:3). Slightly less than two thousand years ago, John on the island of Patmos was summoned to look into heaven's own throne room, and there he saw angels flying around the throne of God, crying out in ceaseless praise: "Holy, holy, holy is the Lord God Almighty, who was, and is, and is to come," (Revelation 4:8). There is an obvious pattern!

Now, presumably the angels who are privileged to exist in the very throne room of the Lord God Almighty know how to praise him. And, from the time of Isaiah to John, the fundamental core of this heavenly hymn of praise has not changed. It should be highly instructive to us that in God's very presence, in the place where he manifests himself as the enthroned sovereign king over the entire universe, his angelic courtiers ceaselessly and repetitiously extol his almighty power and eternal nature, *by three times enunciating his holiness*. They are emphatically proclaiming that God is *holy*. The three-fold repetition is not only for emphasis, but also because the number three is symbolic of completion or perfection in biblical imagery. Thus, the angels are ceaselessly worshiping God because he is completely, totally, and utterly holy.

Granting the importance of God's holiness, then, it becomes obvious that it is exceptionally important for us to understand what it means to be holy. The governing idea behind the Hebrew understanding of "holy" is that of "separation," or "being cut apart." If I were to take a book and cut it in half, I would have two separate pieces. I could take one of the pieces and "set it apart" from the other one. When God called Israel to be a holy nation, he "cut them out" of the other nations or "set them apart." Basically, this means that God made a distinction between the nation of Israel and the other nations around them. They were to be different, distinct, set apart, *holy*. In the tabernacle there was a shovel which was called "holy." How can a shovel be considered holy? Well, the shovel was considered holy because it was set apart from common use and reserved only for the work of shoveling out the ashes from the altar of burnt offerings. It was set apart for the work of the tabernacle; it was not to be used for gardening.

Perhaps the most common usage of "holiness" in today's Christian vocabulary is ethical in nature. That is, we are to abstain from everything that is impure, and we are to grow in holy living. Paul discusses this concept of holiness in II Corinthians 6:14-7:1. The idea is that, since we live in a world permeated by sin, if we are to demonstrate our calling out of the world by God, we will live in a way which is very different from the unregenerate people around us. Since the world is marked by rampant sin and ungodliness, we will demonstrate that we have been set apart by God by our moral purity. As we "come out," or are "separated," from all kinds of evil practices, we will be showing that we are truly called out of the world by God. This does not mean never watching a movie, or speaking in "Thees" and "Thous." It does mean, however, that during our lives we should be transparently becoming less and less like the world, and more and more like God himself.

The command for Christians to be holy is grounded in the holiness of God. This connection is made evident by Peter, when he writes: "But just as he who called you is holy, so be holy in all you do; for it is written, 'Be holy, because I am holy,'" (I Peter 1:15-16). Since God is morally set apart from all sin, we are to be morally set apart from sin, too. Sin is cut away from God; it is not found in him at all. As God's children, we are to be like him in this regard. Just as God is completely separated from sin, we are to strive to be as separate from sin as possible.

The moral dimension of holiness is very important, but it is not all that God's holiness entails. Just like the shovel in the tabernacle was "holy" but not "moral," God's holiness encompasses more than just morality. In essence, God's holiness denotes the fact that he is radically separate from all things in a transcendent sense. The angels in his presence are without sin, but God is still holy or set apart from them. He is the majestic and infinite Other. He is a self-existent, eternal, and infinite person, existing as absolute moral splendor and perfection. He is the great Creator; everything else that exists is finite, derivative, and totally dependent on him. The Creator/creature distinction by itself ensures that God is set apart from all things, but when we add to this distinction the difference between God's sinless holiness and our sinful wickedness, the gap is so inconceivably large in both an ontological and ethical sense that our understanding hits a brick wall. We are brought back to the LORD, the great "I AM WHO I AM"; and we are on holy ground.

2. Righteous

Some things are right and some things are wrong. When you do the right thing you act *right*eously. Regrettably, we all know what it is like to fail to do what is right, and to actively do what is wrong. In a special, legal context, the word "righteous" refers to legal innocence. If you are on trial in a court of law, and the judge renders a verdict of innocence, you are considered righteous in the eyes of the judge, and thus in the eyes of the law. "Righteous" then can be the opposite of doing something ethically "wrong," or it can be the opposite of "guilty." Either way, being righteous as opposed to unrighteous is always the best position to be in.

God, not surprisingly, is perfectly righteous. He has never done, nor will he ever do, anything wrong. Everything God has ever done has, by definition, been right. Furthermore, God always does that which is right because his underlying character is completely righteous. For sinful human beings, when we do unrighteous things it is because we are naturally disposed to do wrong. Character precedes action. Bad character produces bad or unrighteous behavior, while good character produces good or righteous behavior. God is righteous in all of his ways because his character is perfectly and morally *right*. There is a sense in which we can truly say that God is righteous because he is righteous (i.e., God always exalts and glorifies that which is perfect—namely himself—which is always the right attitude to have and always results in doing that which is right). He will forever remain righteous, and forever act righteously, because his nature is fundamentally and essentially righteous. In other words, God will never do anything wrong, and he will persist in doing what is right (and so never become unrighteous) because right-ness is bound up with who he is.

To forestall an objection, God in his sovereignty is in control of all things (including evil and physical disasters) and yet he still always acts righteously. In fact, it is *because* he is righteous that God sends disasters. In Daniel 9:14 we read: "The Lord did not hesitate to bring disaster upon us, for the Lord our God is righteous in everything he does; yet we have not obeyed him." Here, the Lord's righteousness is the very reason that he sends disasters. The only possible answer to Abraham's question, "Will not the Judge of all the earth do right?" (Genesis 18:25c) is an unqualified, "of course he will; he can do nothing else."

3. Just

There is a tight connection between God's righteousness and justice. Both of these themes come together beautifully in Deuteronomy 32:4: "He is the Rock, his works are perfect, and all his ways are just. A faithful God who does no wrong, upright and just is he." Everything God does is perfect and just. He never does, and in fact he cannot do, anything wrong. Again, this is because of his perfect moral character.

God the just is the judge of the universe. Every single person will stand before his judgment seat one day to hear God's verdict about their lives. Since God is omniscient, he cannot be deceived or tricked. God does not need witnesses, since God is the perfect eye-witness to everything that has ever happened. He does not need the prosecution to establish a probable motive, because God knows not only *what* we have done but *why* we have done it. There will not be, and cannot be, a mistrial or a miscarriage of justice. The full rigor and demands of justice will be satisfied on that day.

This should be both comforting and terrifying. The good news is that nobody gets away with it, but that's the bad news too! Every one of us stands justly condemned at the bar of God's justice. Yet, at the same time, the only hope sinners have is in the full, uncompromising justice of God. If God is not completely just, there can be no good news or gospel at all. The next two chapters will explore the logic of the gospel, and the place of God's holy and righteous justice in it.

4. Love

"God is love," (I John 4:16b). If there is one thing people seem to believe about God, it is that he is loving. But God's love is terribly misconstrued. It is too often detached from his holy, righteous, and just character. It is elevated to the place of theological control, and then defined to be little more than deep sentimentality. "God is love," people quote, but they fail to mention that the Lord God Almighty is "holy, holy, holy." This type of misunderstanding is clearly demonstrated by the people who say things such as: "God could never send people to hell because he is too loving to do such a thing." Or, "God could never be sovereign, because a loving God would not allow me to suffer." Such statements reflect a profound misunderstanding of the nature of God. We love love, so we are prone to magnify it to the point of distortion. We naturally hate righteousness, so we are prone to diminish it or dismiss it altogether. Neither attitude is sufficient, because neither attitude encapsulates the biblical teaching on the subject. Yes, God is love, but like all of his other characteristics, God's love must be understood in the terms of his self-revelation.

One major way that God's love is expressed in the Old Testament is by his continually acting in the best interests of his covenant people. He sets his love upon the nation of Israel, and enters into a covenant relationship with them (cf., Deuteronomy 7:7-11). Because he loves them, he will do what is best for them—including punishing them and reducing them to exiles when they persist in flagrant rebellion against him. Yet, in his love for them, he will do all that is required by his covenant bonds. Love for God is more about concrete actions than emotional feelings. As the stronger covenant partner he *acts* to help the weaker partner. When we love our enemies it is a reflection of the love of the Lord who blesses even the wicked with sun and rain (cf., Matthew 6:43ff). It is precisely when we don't *feel* like doing something that genuine love moves us to action. I may not be able to emotionally well up warm feelings towards the person who hates me and persecutes me, but in love I can pray for them, and do good to them as opportunity arises.

5. Faithful

There are times when even the staunchest follower of the Lord can grow weary and discouraged. In the life of Moses, when he came down from Mount Sinai after being given the law from the hand of the Lord, he discovered that in his absence the nation of Israel had rebelled against the Lord and fallen into debauchery and idolatry. Even his brother Aaron had succumbed to the pressure, and led the people in their apostasy. Moses threw down the stone tablets that the Lord had given him, and a fearful judgment was unleashed upon the people. Afterwards, God told Moses to chisel out another set of stone tablets, and to bring them back up on Mount Sinai. Moses dutifully obeyed, and when he got up on the mountain God passed before him, proclaiming his name, the Lord. He said: "The Lord, the Lord, the compassionate and gracious God, slow to anger, abounding in love and faithfulness, maintaining love to thousands, and forgiving wickedness, rebellion, and sin. Yet he does not leave the guilty unpunished; he punishes the children and their children for the sin of the fathers to the third and fourth generation," (Exodus 34:6-7).

What a comfort for Moses! Yes, God is dreadfully holy, and he cannot tolerate sin. He will not allow the guilty to go unpunished, and the consequences of sin can affect future generations. But he is slow to anger and abounds in love and faithfulness. God is a forgiving God. Moses needed this gracious self-disclosure from God. Perhaps Moses was wondering if the future of Israel could really be bright, after their immense sin against such a holy God. Moses need not fear, because God is abounding in love and faithfulness. God's faithfulness denotes a covenant partner who will never let you down. He can always be relied upon, always trusted, and always depended on. Israel may swear fidelity to the covenant, but their actions will belie their words. God is a faithful covenant partner—he is as good as his word. When God makes a covenant, it is guaranteed that he will keep every stipulation and every obligation.

An analogy is often made by the prophets and apostles between God's covenant partnership and wedding vows. When God enters into a sacred covenant marriage, every word he vows he will perfectly uphold and fulfill. His spouse may fail to honor her vows and fall into spiritual adultery, but God is at all times entirely faithful. Read the Old Testament and ask if God kept his end of the Old Covenant. The answer is yes. Read the New Testament, and ask if God will keep his end of the New Covenant. The answer is yes. Different covenants have different terms and conditions, but every last word and promise in God's covenants will be fulfilled by him. God proved himself to be totally faithful in the Old Covenant—what a blessing to know he will be completely faithful in the far better New Covenant!

6. Gracious/Merciful

I am going to lump two characteristics together in this section for the sake of convenience. Although they are not identical, there is a large overlap between the biblical concepts of grace and mercy. In fact, lexically, some languages do not have two distinct words differentiating these terms. When I was in Northern Uganda speaking at a conference in a remote area, I was privileged to work with two excellent translators. They hardly missed a beat, until I mentioned that God was both gracious and merciful. My interpreter turned to me at that point and said, "We only have one word for those two things." I had to pause for a minute, and then replied, "One word, two meanings." Even though mercy and grace are closely aligned, they can be helpfully differentiated.

At a popular level, *mercy* is often described as withholding something negative from someone that they deserve (e.g., punishment), whereas *grace* is understood to refer to giving something positive to someone that they do not deserve (e.g., rewards). Using this as a rough working model, God in his mercy does not punish sinners as they deserve, and in his grace he blesses them not for their merits, but in spite of their *de*-merits. Even here, however, God's sovereignty comes to the foreground, because he reveals himself to be the God who has mercy on whom he wants to have mercy (cf., Romans 9:15).

A careful reader will perhaps at this point (if not sooner) notice a particular tension developing. God has been described as being holy, righteous, and perfectly just. It has been noted that he will not allow justice to be miscarried, and he will not allow the guilty to go free. If human beings are sinners or law-breakers, however, how can God be merciful and gracious to them? It would seem that God is being deeply inconsistent. He is just, but he withholds punishment. He is righteous, but he blesses the unrighteous. How can this be? The following two chapters will examine this biblical tension, and hopefully it will be made clear that this is an internal tension in God, but not a logical contradiction. Grace and mercy will meet up with justice and righteousness in an amazing way in God's unfolding sovereign plan of salvation.

7. Good

God's goodness is not reducible to "niceness." In today's English, "good" is a pretty bland descriptive, but when used of God, "good" is an awesome word. The whole concept of goodness flows from the God Who Is. God is not good because he is like something else, or some other standard; in fact, other things are only good in a derivative sense, as they reflect God. God is not good because he conforms to an external ideal of pure "goodness." Goodness *itself* only exists as an idea because God exists in the concrete. If God did not exist, not only would there not be anything that was good, but there would not even be such a thing as goodness. When we identify something as good, it is only a correct identification to the extent that it shares, in some way, the character of God. In other words, goodness, value, beauty, morals, and desirousness are only properly understood as overflows of the character of God found in his creation. The entire creation is revelation from God, and so when we find something worthy of desire, or perceive beauty or goodness around us, it is only because God has surrounded us with things that reflect his nature, so that we can come to appreciate his ultimate goodness, beauty, and worth, with fuller wonder, love, and praise.

8. Immutable

From the list of attributes discussed so far in this chapter, "immutable" may seem like a strange fit. The reader may be forgiven for thinking that, as far as my categorization up until this point, this attribute would have been better treated in the previous chapter. I have, however, purposefully left this attribute until now. The reason is that after we reflect on the wonderful character of God, we should sit back and think, "With such a great God, I hope he never changes!"

Thankfully, God cannot change. He is immutable. All around us the world is in constant flux—from the subatomic level to the universe at large, things are constantly changing. Society changes. Fashion changes. People grow, move, and die. Despite all of the external and internal changes that we experience, God never changes. He is an unchanging rock of stability. He is righteous and holy and omniscient today, and he will be that way for all of eternity. Amazingly, this immutable God can interact with mutable creatures. The Lord does not change, but we do, and he has entered into a real, dynamic, and living covenant relationship with us. Immutability is not the same immobility. As hard as some of this may be to understand, the most important thing about God's immutability is that God's wonderful and perfect character will never change!

Summary

God is holy, righteous, and just. He is love. He is good, merciful, faithful, and gracious. And he never changes. Different theologians have drawn up different schemes of God's attributes, and they have also enumerated them differently. These two chapters were not written to be exhaustive or exclusive. Books have been written on each one of the attributes mentioned, and there is still more thinking to be done on every one of them. The aim of these two chapters, however, was to bring the great nature of a great God to the forefront of our minds. It is only when we start with the grandeur of God—the God Who Is in the very beginning—that we will be ready for the next link in the chain of the gospel. This next link will be examined in the following chapter.

Chapter Three

THE FALL INTO SIN

After thinking about the character of God, we are in a better position to consider what we owe him. At the very, very minimum, we owe him tremendous respect. Clearly a being like God deserves to be treated with the utmost reverence. When he speaks, all should pay heed and obey. Since he is the very fountain of purity, righteousness, and goodness, he should be valued and loved above everything else. What God has created can provide us with pleasure and the opportunity for awesome contemplation—how much more so the Creator himself! It should not be forgotten, of course, that our very existence is owing to his power and will. Literally, we owe God all that we are and all that we have. Every joy is ultimately from his hand, and every blessing attained in our existence is owing to his decision to create us and sustain us.

All that God has made—including human beings—is for his glory. The angels in heaven worship God saying: "You are worthy, our Lord and God, to receive glory and honor and power, for you created all things, and by your will they were created and have their being," (Revelation 4:11). It is because it is by God's will that all things were created and are continually sustained that he is worthy to receive glory. His creation *owes* him praise. Not only are all things *from* him and *through* him, they also exist *to* him, or for his sake (cf., Romans 11:36). Summoned out of nothing except the voluntary pleasure of his will, all God's creatures should delight themselves in him, and live in perpetual gratitude and thanksgiving for the work of his hands. Our orientation in life should be to praise the God Who Is—the one who created us with the capacity to know and rejoice in his limitless perfections.

As was noted earlier, God created the universe and its constituent parts by verbal command. He simply speaks, and it is done. He said, "'Let there be light,' and there was light," (Genesis 1:3). As the creative work of God unfolds, it is through the constant repetition of God speaking, and his words bringing forth the desired results. The thoughtful reader should be mightily impressed only a few verses into the Bible, because here is revealed a God who simply is, and whose words are so powerful that they bring a universe and all life into existence *ex nihilo*. With words this efficacious and with results so pristinely good—even *very* good—it would seem that anything this God says should be unconditionally accepted as powerful, good, and true. Should anyone doubt the word of a God whose words are mighty enough to create a very good, harmonious world?

It is precisely at this point, however, that the image bearers of God will be tempted to deny their maker. The serpent comes to them in the garden, and, "He *said* to the woman, 'Did God really *say*, "You must not eat from any tree in the garden"?'" (Gen. 3:1b, emphasis added). The serpent's tactic is to cast doubt on the word of God. He counters God's speech with speech of his own. Now, Adam and Eve knew that God spoke and created the universe, and that he spoke about the forbidden fruit of the tree of the knowledge of good and evil (Gen. 2:17). The God who had commanded light to exist by his verbal power had also used his verbal abilities to command them not to eat from this one tree in the garden. If his former word had brought this good universe into existence, why should they doubt his latter word about the fruit?

As Eve talked with the serpent, the tempter moved from casting doubt on God's word to directly contradicting it. God had said they would die if they ate the fruit from the tree of the knowledge of good and evil, but the serpent says, "You will not surely die," (Gen. 3:4). He has just explicitly claimed that God's word is false. Going further, the serpent asserts that God's word is false because God's character is flawed. The serpent tells Eve that God lied to them when he warned them about dying, "For God knows that when you eat of it your eyes will be opened, and you will be like God, knowing good and evil," (Gen. 3:5).

When we hear the old expression that someone is as good as their word, it means that the person being referred to is trustworthy and dependable. When we are told to "consider the source," it can mean that the source of information is less than reliable, and we need to be wary. Some people are chronically misinformed, others are prone to wild exaggeration, and still others, sadly, are practiced liars. God's word, however, can never be doubted, because his character is perfect. He always speaks the truth; in fact, he *is* truth. He is omniscient and morally flawless. His omnipotent word actualizes his desire to create a universe, and the universe is good.

Why did Adam and Eve fail to obey the word of God? Why did they trust the words of the serpent above the words of the Lord? Why did they listen and act upon the words of a creature, rather than the words of the Creator?

Even if we cannot understand all that happened in the garden, one thing is clear from the effects of their sin: God's word proved to be true. He was as good as his word.

That first act of disobedience brought death into the world. Adam and Eve died spiritually when they became impure in the sight of their perfect Lord and creator. God brought a curse into the world that affected all things, and from then on decay, degeneration, and physical death slowly began to wreak havoc on the earth. All human beings—from that day on—are spiritually dead even while they live; and physical death comes eventually for all. Waiting behind our first physical death is a second, irrevocable, eternal death in hell that looms large on the postmortem horizon for all who have rejected the word of the Lord as Adam and Eve did, by choosing to go their own way. And the message of the Bible is that *everyone* without exception has been born in sin, lives in sin, loves sin, and would rather obey the voice and impulse of their sin nature and the devil than the word of God. Moment by moment human beings repeat the sin of their forebears: they willingly reject the word of God to go their own way.

The apostle Paul articulates this truth with unmistakable strength and clarity in Romans 1:18-32. I will be referencing portions of this passage in the next few pages, but you should stop reading this book now to pick up a copy of the Bible. Read this section in Romans, and then resume reading this chapter with an open Bible. After all, the Scriptures are the word of God, and if we are to learn something from Adam and Eve, it is that God's word must be accepted and taken to heart over the words of anyone else.

The Fall Into Sin

Just before moving into verse 18, however, I would like to back up and look at verses 16-17. In these two verses Paul writes: "I am not ashamed of the gospel, because it is the power of God for the salvation of everyone who believes: first for the Jew, then for the Gentile. For in the gospel a righteousness from God is revealed, a righteousness that is by faith from first to last, just as it is written: 'The righteous will live by faith.'"

It will be the task of the next chapter to explore how this gospel actually works, but for now a few preliminary comments will suffice.

First, the gospel is the power of God for the salvation of anyone and everyone who simply believes it, whether they are Jews or Gentiles (those two categories included everyone on earth; i.e., Jews and everyone else). Second, God has revealed "a righteousness." This righteousness is from him. It is not earned by human beings, or forged on the anvil of their good works. For, in the third place, Paul emphasizes the fact that this righteousness is not only by faith, it is *totally* by faith, from beginning to end, first to last. The righteous can only live by faith.

What would we expect Paul to say immediately after writing these two verses? Perhaps he will launch into a tribute to God's love or grace. Maybe he will talk about all the blessings that belong to the believer in Christ Jesus. That would be very fitting, except for one thing: Paul is writing this letter to *explain* the heart of the gospel. Why does God need to supply us with righteousness? Why does it need to be by faith from first to last? From 1:18-3:20, Paul is going to prove beyond a shadow of a doubt that every single human being is a miserable rebel against God, deserving of nothing more than destruction and damnation. Until this point is hammered into our hardened hearts and minds, the gospel of salvation cannot make sense, nor can its necessity be grasped.

As we have noted, in 1:17 Paul writes that in the gospel "a righteousness from God is revealed." In verse 18, Paul notes that something else is being revealed too—namely the wrath of Almighty God. God's wrath is being revealed against "all the godlessness and wickedness of men." Follow the logic of God's wrath:

1. Godless and wicked men are *suppressing the truth* by their wickedness (v. 18)

2. They are suppressing the plain knowledge of God that they have (v. 19)

3. From the beginning of creation, God's power and nature have been *clearly seen* (v. 20)

4. So all men are without excuse (v. 20)

5. For they knew God, but did not glorify him or even give him thanks (v. 21)

6. They thought they knew more than God, but they were fools (v. 21-22)

7. They traded the glory of God the Creator for the images of the creation (v. 23)

8. Therefore, God gave them over to their wickedness, and they were trapped by it (v. 24)

9. They exchanged *truth* for a *lie* (v. 25)

10. Instead of worshiping the Creator, they worship what God made (v. 25)

11. Since this is what they wanted, they spiraled down in increasing debauchery (v. 26)

The Fall Into Sin

12. They fell so far they even perverted the natural order they tried to worship (v. 26)

13. Because they did not think the knowledge of God was *worthwhile*, God:

> "gave them over to a depraved mind, to do what ought not to be done. They have become filled with every kind of wickedness, evil, greed and depravity. They are full of envy, murder, strife, deceit and malice. They are gossips, slanderers, God-haters, insolent, arrogant and boastful; they invent ways of doing evil; they disobey their parents; they are senseless, faithless, heartless, ruthless." (v. 28-31)

14. They *know* that those who do these things *deserve* death (v. 32)

15. But they keep doing them, and encourage others to do them too (v. 32).

A holy and just God *must* be filled with wrath when he surveys such gross immorality and flagrant wickedness. As a perfect judge, his verdict by definition is completely correct—and his verdict is that all who live this way (which is inclusive of all people) *deserve death.*

The symptoms of rebellion are found in such things as gossip, murder, arrogance, disobedience to parents, sexual immorality, greed, deceit, etc. It is easy to gloss over many of the items in this list, because they seem so random. After all, we all burn against injustice and murder, but certainly little lies aren't that bad! According to God, the greedy are lumped together with the murderers; and furthermore, they all deserve death.

The disease itself, however, that is responsible for producing these symptoms is the rejection of the knowledge of God. What may be known about God has been plainly seen from the beginning. In fact, human beings "knew God" but did not honor him *as* God. They decided they would rather bow down to the images of animals rather than to the God in whose image they had been made. Since they were the image bearers of God, when they began to worship the images of the created order, they destroyed their self-understanding. Humans are supposed to find their identity as the image bearers of the one they worship: when they worship the images of animals, they become animalistic. In fact they go beyond this, because they have inverted the natural order by preferring the worship of animals to the worship of God, and in so doing they have sinned against nature itself. Nature is not meant to be worshiped; worshiping it destroys what it really is. So as human beings persisted in rejecting God to worship what God made, they ended up sinning against nature itself. In the end, they even fell into sins which are transparently opposed to the natural order. We are so wicked we even rebel against our idols.

The truth, of course, is that only God is worthy of worship. Only God is worth praising and living for. Only God knows how we should live, and what is best for us. "On the day you eat of it you will surely die," is proved to be true time and again. What is the result of rejecting God? People are idolaters and fools, who love lies instead of truth, and creation instead of the Creator. People sin against God, others, and even themselves, introducing pain wherever they go. Societal, familial, and international conflicts attest to the grim reality that our way is not better than God's way. God spoke, and he gave us a very good world; we willfully and knowingly rejected his world order, and

The Fall Into Sin

plunged it into a place of disorder, hatred, moral vertigo, and death.

Still, we suppress the truth of God. We defend ourselves, and argue that while some people may deserve death, we do not. As if the sociopath convicts on death row are in a position to adjudicate what's right and wrong! We are death row moral philosophers, arguing that our conviction is unjust. Surely we know what we deserve! One murder is acceptable. Only those who torture their victim first should die. Adultery is fine, provided it is done with love, etc., etc. Throughout all of our rationalizing one conclusion is always reached: I do not deserve punishment, because I am either innocent or deserve to be excused on the basis of special considerations.

No, God—the perfect judge—is the only one in a position to truly know what punishment fits the crime. Our minds and consciences are so defiled that we justify dark acts and condemn the pure ones. Yet, on a deeper level a suppressed truth is stifled but not muted. It takes effort for us to push away the knowledge of God, and it takes practice to sear our consciences. In quiet moments without distraction, we may hear the quiet voice of truth crying out to us, and we may feel our guilt. But another drink, some internet surfing, or an exercise in rationalizing away our faults seem to do the trick—for a time.

If you are to understand the logic of the gospel you must come face to face with your total depravity and wickedness. You must know that you are an object of God's just wrath. How great is his wrath? God's "wrath is as great as the fear that is due [him]" (Psalm 90:11b). In other words, God's wrath is in direct proportion to his greatness: the very greatness we have rejected as unworthy of our time and attention.

Here is when it is helpful to rehearse the glorious attributes of God that we briefly discussed in the first two chapters. God is infinitely awesome, and infinitely worthy of worship, praise, and reverence. His wrath is as high as his character. His wrath is equal to the amount of worship he deserves. Since we have withheld from him worship, and we have rejected him and despised him, his wrath is greater than we can possibly imagine.

Just in case we hold onto the vain hope that somehow we are excluded from this list of sinners, Paul cites some Old Testament passages that prove the universal guilt of every human being. He quotes: "There is no one righteous, not even one; there is no one who understands, no one who seeks God. All have turned away, they have together become worthless; there is no one who does good, not even one," (Rom. 3:10b-12). There is not even *one* who is righteous. *All* are worthless. There is *no one* good—and in case you missed it, let it be said again—*not even one*.

The main point is that every last person on earth has failed to be righteous and deserves death. Every last person lives under the wrath of God. In ourselves, there is no hope at all. We have nothing to look forward to but death and hell, and there is not a single thing we can do to change our standing before God. We have culpably rebelled, we have lived foolish and miserable lives, and our future is worse than the present. Precisely what part of this is the good news?

Chapter Four

SALVATION IN JESUS CHRIST

The good news is built on the foundation of the bad news. Although there is no hope *in* us, there is hope *for* us. After reading the first few chapters of Romans, we cannot possibly think that God can tolerate our wickedness, or that sin will go unpunished. We cannot—as much as we would like to—exonerate ourselves from God's holy justice and wrath. The charges against us are proven, and the penalty deserved is death. On the basis of our attitudes, words, deeds, and lives, we are justly damned. God's justice must be satisfied, and the soul that sins must die (Ezekiel 18:20).

"But now," Paul says, "a righteousness from God, apart from law, has been made known, to which the Law and the Prophets testify. This righteousness from God comes through faith in Jesus Christ to all who believe. There is no difference, for all have sinned and fall short of the glory of God," (Romans 3:21-23). Observe the logic of Paul's argument:

First, after fully detailing the hopeless state and unrighteous filthiness of every human being, Paul says that there is a righteousness *from* God. Paul had previously said that in the gospel "a righteousness from God is revealed," (Rom. 1:17), and here he tells us that this righteousness comes after the human race has been plunged into a flood of sin and dissipation. God's creatures traded away his glory and truth, and fully rejected him—but now, after all this, he still is going to help us. All that we have is unrighteousness; the righteousness he offers is exactly what we need. Since it is a righteousness *from* God, it must be a righteousness that is acceptable *to* God. As the perfect judge, God knows what passes his perfect standard. In order to qualify as "righteous" a person must be righteous enough to meet the standard of God's perfection. If God provides "righteousness," it is "righteous" indeed.

Second, this righteousness from God is not earned by our works. On the contrary, "it comes through faith in Jesus Christ to all who believe." Romans 1:17 introduces the gospel as the news that God has revealed a righteousness which is by faith from first to last. More will be said at the end of this chapter about what it means to have faith in Jesus Christ. At this point it will suffice to say that it is the opposite of having faith in ourselves. Rather than rejecting God to rely on ourselves, we reject our own righteousness and entrust ourselves fully to God through Jesus Christ. It involves a recognition that only Jesus is righteous, and we are not. It involves repenting or turning away from sin, and submitting all that we are to God. It is saying: "Lord, in myself there is the corruption and death of a sinner. I deserve nothing but death and hell. In justice I am guilty, and in justice I deserve everything you say I deserve. But there is a righteousness you offer that has come through Jesus Christ, and I need it—it is my only hope."

Third, this righteousness is not required for some people and not for others. *All* have sinned and deserve death; *all* have fallen short of God's glory. If *anyone* is to be declared righteous, it is only by receiving the righteousness that has come down from God. There is no exception on the basis of ethnicity, age, sex, language, economic position, culture, or

Salvation in Jesus Christ 47

other environmental factors. All have fallen short, but all who believe in Jesus Christ will receive this gift of righteousness.

What Paul says next is of the utmost importance, and it represents the heart of the gospel. Even though the entire human race has culpably rebelled against God in a manner which defies description, human beings can be "justified freely by his grace," (v.24a). To be *justified* means to be pronounced *just*. It is a legal concept. The same sinners who deserve death can stand before the judgment seat of God and be pronounced legally innocent. Furthermore, this legal justification is not purchased by a bribe, nor does it come through a mistrial. It comes without any cost to us (i.e., "freely") and it is completely undeserved (i.e., "by grace"). Sinners can be justified by the free grace of a sovereign God: But how?

Next we are told that this justification comes "through the redemption that came by Christ Jesus," (v.24b). To be *redeemed* means to be bought back—and the original context is being bought back out of slavery. When God brought the nation of Israel out of the land of Egypt where they had been slaves for more than 400 years, God acted to "redeem" them. This event becomes the prototypical image for what redemption is all about. His people are helplessly mired in slavery, so God acts with sovereign grace and power to free the captives. This physical redemption from national slavery is a picture that points forward to the greatest redemption that could ever come to a sinful race: redemption and freedom from slavery to sin and death and judgment. The greatest act of redemption comes by Christ

Jesus, as he buys his people from sin and death, and freely justifies them.

Redemption was secured when, "God presented him [Jesus] as a sacrifice of atonement, through faith in his blood," (v. 25a). It may be better to translate the phrase "sacrifice of atonement" by using the word "propitiation." *Propitiation* means to make favorable, and Jesus does this by satisfying the wrath of God that figures so prominently in the first chapter of Romans. Because of his holy and just nature God is full of wrath against godlessness and wickedness—and any other response would be unworthy of God's matchless character. God's justice demands satisfaction. If justice is not satisfied than God is not just, which would be a denial of his very nature. Yet Jesus willingly substitutes himself into the place of his people, and he bears the penalty of justice for their sake. This concept requires more attention.

Jesus Christ is fully God and fully man. He has all the characteristics of deity, and he joined his deity to human nature. Jesus was born without sin, and he lived his entire life always pleasing God. Since Jesus never sinned, he had no sins for which he could die. God was fully satisfied with the perfect righteousness of Jesus. Yet Jesus willingly chose to die and to suffer the wrath of God. He did this so that God's justice could be satisfied and the penalty of the law would be paid, but at the same time God would be able to pour out his love and grace and mercy upon his people. (As a matter of fact, the cross happens *because* of the love, grace, and mercy of God. If God was not loving and merciful, the program of salvation would never have even begun.) The plan of the cross, where Jesus dies in the place of his people, paying for their sins, exalts the wrath, justice, holiness, righteousness, love, mercy, and grace of God, and everything else that he is. On the cross Jesus brings the fullest display of the character of God that has ever been seen.

The atonement provided by Jesus has its roots in the Old Testament sacrificial system. One day a year, on the Day of Atonement, two goats were used in an event which set forth in a figurative way what was required to bring sinful men together with the God they had sinned against. The first goat had the sins of the people symbolically confessed over its head, and in so doing the sin was "transferred" to the goat. This goat was led far out into the wilderness and abandoned. God was teaching the people through this image that sin had to be *expiated* or "removed." In order to be with God the people could not be bearing their own sin. They needed to be purified, but the problem was they were hopelessly fallen and defiled. Their sin needed to be put on a substitute, who would bear it away from them, leaving them pure.

The second goat also had a part to play in this drama. He was offered on an altar as a burnt sacrifice. His destruction by fire symbolized the fact that God must pour out his wrath on sin. God could not simply ignore it or let the guilty go free. Sin must be punished, and the penalty of sin is death. It was the goat who symbolically bore the punishment of sin, and was destroyed by the holy justice of God. This picture helped the people see that God's wrath was real; total destruction was the consequence of sin; and unless their sin was transferred to a substitute, they would bear the wrath of God and be destroyed in like manner.

Atonement, then, includes these twin elements of expiation and propitiation, or purification and satisfaction. At its very core it also requires a substitute. Only an innocent person could pay the penalty for a guilty one, since each guilty individual has to die *for their own* sins. Take as an example two people who commit heinous murders, and who are both sentenced to the death penalty. One of them could not say to the judge: "Listen, I'll die for that person over there." The judge would reply: "You can't die for him. Yes, you will die, but your death only satisfies the justice of this court for your crime. That person must die as well, or justice will not have been done." If you are sentenced to die, you cannot die for someone else as well. Since every sinner stands deserving the death sentence for their own sins, a sinner could not possibly satisfy justice by dying for someone else. A real substitute for sinners would by definition have to be perfectly innocent and righteous. And this is precisely what Jesus Christ is—he is perfectly righteous.

The remainder of Rom. 3:25-26 teaches that God did this to prove that he was just in fellowshipping with sinners in the past. It looked like God was being unjust by treating sinners with grace, but his grace in the past was grounded in the certain knowledge that Jesus was going to provide a real atonement. The goats were a picture of atonement, but Jesus' death on the cross was the real thing. Jesus Christ acted so perfectly in his life and death that God remained just, and was able to justify his people, who would put their faith in Jesus Christ.

It is only against this total gospel backdrop that the resurrection of Jesus from the dead makes sense. When Jesus died on the cross he died under the curse of God. How

Salvation in Jesus Christ

could somebody who was cursed by God be considered the savior? Jesus really died, and was really buried. What did a dead savior prove? Well, after Jesus' death God raised him from the dead. Jesus truly died as a substitute for sinners, and since he died for them, God raised him from the dead to demonstrate that Jesus' life had been perfect. On the basis of his merits Jesus earned eternal life, and on the basis of his substitutionary sacrifice he paid the full penalty for the sins of his people. Since his death was for others, and since his death was a completely successful atonement, God raised him from the dead. Death was the penalty, and Jesus paid it. Jesus had earned life, and had traded it away. In his death God treated Jesus as if he was a sinner, but in the resurrection God treated Jesus as he really deserved.

Now is the proper time to ask the question about the relationship between Christ's work on the cross and faith. This gospel is by faith from first to last, Paul said, and the righteousness that is from God comes through faith. What does it mean to have faith in Jesus, and why is this faith so necessary?

Faith is necessary because it involves totally entrusting oneself to God. It is, in some ways, the inverse of the first sin. Adam and Eve brought sin and death into the world by not putting their faith in the words and character of God. We are saved by what Christ did objectively on our behalf, and by fully committing ourselves to the truth of the gospel. Faith receives what God has provided as 100% sufficient, whereas the opposite of faith requires us to try to earn our way into God's heaven. As Paul makes clear, this second option is impossible. Faith is resting in God's grace through Jesus Christ. It is acknowledging our sinfulness, acknowledging that we have no hope, acknowledging that we deserve death, and *acknowledging that in spite of ourselves, God has made a way through the atonement of Jesus Christ for us to be saved.* Emptying ourselves and casting ourselves on God's mercy is our only option for justification. But when we have faith in God's word, and we come to understand what God is like, and when the Holy Spirit reveals to us the glorious truth of the gospel…well, there is nothing else to do but to joyfully receive the good news of salvation.

It is at this juncture that one more foundational issue emerges. In the last chapter we saw that the real problem with human beings is not so much what they do as it is their heart that motivates them to do evil. We do not just do wicked things; we are wicked beings. Sin naturally flows from our fallen and corrupted nature, and we love it that way. Sinners hate God. They will not worship him; they cannot submit to him. Darkness is loved and light is hated. People are not ignorant of the existence and nature of God: they willfully suppress God's truth because they do not consider God worthwhile to know. Jesus provided a perfect atonement on the cross, and all who believe and put their faith in him will be saved. *But nobody will believe* because of their wicked hearts, for which there is no cure. Let me provide a short list of texts that underscore this point. All emphasis in the following quotations is mine.

1. Genesis 8:21b. "Never again will I curse the ground because of man, even though *every inclination of his heart is evil from childhood.*" (God makes this pronouncement after Noah comes off the ark at the end of the flood. Even after

Salvation in Jesus Christ 53

the flood, the human race is characterized by universal and radical sinfulness.)

2. Jeremiah 17:9-10. "The heart is deceitful *above all things* and beyond cure. Who can understand it? I the Lord search the heart and examine the mind, to reward a man according to his conduct, according to what his deeds deserve." (There is nothing more wicked than the heart, and it cannot be cured. The heart is so deceitful we cannot even understand it. God searches our hearts and minds, he sees what we do, and he gives us what our deeds deserve—which, as Paul said, is death.)

3. John 3:19-20. "This is the verdict: Light has come into the world, but men *loved darkness* instead of light *because their deeds were evil*. Everyone who does evil hates the light, and *will not come into the light* for fear that his deeds will be exposed." (Jesus [the Light] came into the world, but sinners loved darkness, and so they rejected him. They do not, and will not, come into the light.)

To this short representative sample of Bible verses we could add the fact that humans are "dead in trespasses and sin," (Ephesians 2:1-2), and the fact that the human mind "is hostile to God" and furthermore it *"cannot submit to God's law,"* (Romans 8:7). Earlier in Romans Paul argued that failure to honor and submit to God is at the heart of sin, but in this verse he argues that the unregenerate human mind *cannot* submit to God. What we have is an absolutely hopeless situation. Humans are entirely sinful. They cannot submit to God. Failure to submit to God deserves death. (When people say that God cannot exist because there is too much suffering in the world, they prove they know nothing about what they deserve. They deserve death and no pleasure at all, rather than a pain-free life.) Deep down every human being knows this to be true, but because they love darkness and hate the light, they do their best to deceive themselves about their true state. Being dead in sin, hating God, loving evil, and not being able to submit to God's laws guarantees that, in themselves, humans are entirely lost, without any hope at all. *There is not one shred of hope for any sinner in and of themselves.* Every single person stands justly condemned before the holy judge and ruler of all things. Every single person is guilty. We have no excuse, no justification, no reason; we have nothing to say. We are guilty, and we are condemned. And we hate God too much to ever want anything to do with his gift of righteousness.

What happens behind the scenes when people put their faith in Jesus Christ is described by Luke when he was inspired by God to write the account of the conversion of a woman named Lydia. Luke writes in Acts 16:14b: "The Lord opened her heart to respond to Paul's message." Since she was a sinner, Lydia's heart needed to be opened by God before she could *respond* to Paul's message. Whenever someone puts their faith in Jesus Christ, it is because of this prior work of God, sometimes called "regeneration." It is the same reality as that which is described by Jesus when he says that a sinner "must be born again," (cf., John 3:1-8). When we are born we are passive. When someone is born again it is owing to the mysterious, sovereign work of the Holy Spirit in their life. In John 3 Jesus is probably alluding to a famous Old Testament passage, and that passage is found in Ezekiel 36:24-32. Again let me suggest that you open your Bible to this passage for the full effect, but I will outline some of the verses to give the general flow of the argument.

God is speaking through Ezekiel to the Israelites, and he says: "I will sprinkle clean water on you, and you will be clean….I will give you a new heart and put a new spirit in you; I will remove from you your heart of stone….I will put my Spirit in you to move you to follow my decrees….I will be your God….I will save you from all your uncleanness….Then you will remember your evil ways and wicked deeds, and you will loathe yourselves for your sins and detestable practices." When do the people hate their sin? They do not receive a new heart by repenting. They do not hate their sins and turn to God, prior to his work in their lives. They are not given the Spirit because of their repentance. No, it is *after* God makes them clean, *after* God gives them a new heart, *after* God gives them his Spirit, *then*—and only *then*—will the people hate their sin and trust in God.

Our hearts are desperately wicked, and there is no hope in us, not even the hope of being good enough to turn to God by faith. God provided salvation through Christ, and God must provide us with a new heart, an opened heart, so that we can respond to the message of the gospel and receive Jesus Christ by faith. Ephesians 2:8-9 says: "For it is by grace you have been saved, through faith—and this not from yourselves, it is the gift of God—not by works, so that no one can boast." We are only saved by God's grace through faith, and *none* of this comes from us; it is *all* the gift of God. The grace that saves is the gift of God, and the faith by which we appropriate this grace is the gift of God as well. Salvation is from the Lord from beginning to end.

Please do not misunderstand. Yes, we exercise faith when we trust Jesus. Yes, we do, like Lydia, respond to the message. But we will only respond the right way to the message if God first opens our heart. And we will only exercise faith in Jesus if we have faith in the first place—and we do not have faith, unless God gives it to us as a free gift. The message of the gospel is that God provided a sacrifice, God provided an atonement, Jesus is the redeemer of his people, and God opens their hearts so they can trust in him, by his grace and for his glory. Jesus is the only hope of sinners, and he is their hope because God is a God of saving grace—and saving grace can only be sovereign grace.

Chapter Five

A SAVING SALVATION

Christ's full atonement for sin means that the sins of his people are expiated or removed from them, and that God's holy justice and wrath are satisfied. This is certainly a good beginning! Yet there is more to the story. When we stand before the judgment seat of God, we are not merely *neutral* in our standing (by virtue of Christ having removed everything *negative* from our account), we have a *positive* standing. The same principle (called imputation) which allows our sins to be transferred to Christ's account allows his righteousness to be transferred to ours. Christ not only took our sin upon himself, but he also gave his spotless righteousness to us. When we stand before God, then, we appear as righteous as Jesus. I say this with the highest fear and reverence that I can: Jesus Christ can no more be condemned to hell than any of his people can be, *because they are as righteous as he is in the sight of God*. All those who repent of their sins and put their faith in Jesus Christ are covered eternally by this saving salvation. The redeemed are eternally secure, eternally purified, and will be eternally giving glory to God, and eternally loving the Lord God with all of their (renewed) hearts, minds, souls, and strength. Genuine salvation is eternal salvation from sin and all the consequences of the curse. (In heaven there is no more death, sorrow, disease, or pain, because the disease which causes these symptoms—sin—is removed forever.)

This accent on future glory in heaven has been one of the hallmarks of Christian theology, and rightly so. How could such a promise fail to grip the heart and mind of every believer? We look forward to summer vacations (if we have the time and finances); how could we not look forward to heaven? There every believer will see Jesus, and every believer will be constituted in such a way that it will be impossible for them to ever sin again. Such themes of glory, worship, sinless purity, unity, peace (i.e., deep, underlying harmony and "rightness" in order), and the presence of Almighty God and the Lamb, simply must occupy our thoughts if we are truly saved. It is the time when the redemptive work of Jesus Christ is brought to its consummation.

Having this state of affairs to look forward to, however, is not meant to reduce our earthly existence to drudgery, boredom, and lazy apathy. In actual fact, the very opposite is the case. Although the consummation of glory awaits Christ's return, there is a sense in which the glory of the future age is flowing backwards into this one. Or, to reverse the stream, the nearer we draw to standing before Christ Jesus our Lord, the more we should be experiencing foretastes of his glory. We will worship God there—let us worship him here. We will be sinless there—let us mortify sin and pursue righteousness here. We will love God and others purely there—let us grow in love for God and others here. We will enjoy peace, harmony, and unity in our relationships with God, his people, and creation there—let us strive for such experiences here. No, we do not passively wait and bide our time here, because we will not do that there.

A Saving Salvation

The salvation given us is most definitely for the future, but that does not mean that it is not also for the present. Salvation is so comprehensive that its outworking takes up all of eternity future, and it also takes up all of our earthly lives. This one world and this short life are the place and time in which the redeemed praise and serve the Lord while surrounded and infiltrated by sin and the curse. Now is the time when we praise God through pain and loss. Now is the time when we walk by faith and not by sight. Now is the time when we share the saving gospel with the lost. Now is *the only time in which we will be able to do these things.*

What does the Christian message do when it is brought into direct confrontation with a rebellious and damned world order? How do redeemed sinners respond to the external and internal wickedness that plagues them? Can weak and frail sinners actually be kept faithful to the end by the power of the Holy Spirit and the gospel of Jesus Christ? Is Christian salvation worth keeping when it results in suffering, persecution, imprisonment, or death? Is Christ worthy to be known and loved, even if such a commitment brings the scorn, hate, and rejection of friends and family? It is here and now, this side of the consummation, that such questions are asked and answered.

Although the following is not going to be exhaustive, it is meant to be somewhat representative and suggestive. My aim is to briefly mention four of the categories in which the saving gospel saves us here and now. More could be added to the ones I will mention, and certainly far more detail could be added to every category discussed. It will have to suffice, however, to note that this chapter contains only a partial list; more could be enumerated. Furthermore, it is of critical importance to recognize that the gospel really does affect *everything in existence*. The fact that I am identifying particular spheres where gospel transformation takes place does not mean that the gospel's impact is somehow limited. There is also another sense in which these four areas are rather arbitrarily selected, and represent some of the concerns of my own time and culture. Nevertheless, there is another sense in which these four areas are perpetual concerns and are of large-scale importance to everyone. (Even if some people are not fully conscious of the importance of these areas, they are still affected by them.)

1. Ecology

Ecological concerns occupy an uncertain place in much of today's evangelicalism. Some churches, concerned with undue, radical environmentalism, have simply been mute about everything green. Others have swung to the other side of the pendulum, and skewered their priorities so that the "good news" is more about fresh air and clean water than about reconciliation with Almighty God through the atoning sacrifice of Jesus Christ on the cross. Many—as in all spectrums—reside somewhere in the middle, perhaps unsure what to do, but certainly not unconcerned. Such issues in today's society are supercharged with the added dynamics of political debate. What, then, is the thoughtful Christian supposed to think?

First, the Christian recognizes that no human being owes anything to the environment *per se*. If the universe is naturalistic, and we are its products, it makes no sense to personify the environment, as if it is a personal being that we

A Saving Salvation

are damaging. Yes, we do owe a tremendous debt concerning our environment—but we owe it to God. The earth is the Lord's. He made it, he was pleased to call it into existence, and he was pleased to fill it with all the necessities for our lives. He then commissioned us to be his stewards over creation. This functioned well in Eden, where the man and the woman cultivated and took care of nature. They did so out of wonder and gratitude to God. They were conscious that they were handling someone else's property. Beyond this, *they themselves*, as part of the created order, were God's property, too.

Second, human beings plunged the world into sin, and brought the curse of God upon the earth. God subjected the created order to futility, and it will be redeemed with the people of God. This state of affairs is the result of sin, and humans are responsible for sin. Are humans today responsible for the damage done to the environment? Yes, of course we are.

Third, modern nations are somewhat like little children "weeding" in someone else's garden. After having been told not to rip up the roses, this is precisely what they did. Then to "fix" the problem they planted weeds. Then they tried to pull the weeds, and although their efforts were sincere, they actually succeeded in doing little more than uprooting the tulips. To which, of course, they responded by planting dandelions. Our ongoing rejection of God's ways is bringing disaster and creating crises at every turn. Just as soon as we think we have solved one problem, we find that we have created another.

The Bible makes clear that there is a correlation between disobedience and natural futility. God is very patient, but when sinners persist in ignoring his ways, he allows them to reap a harvest of futility. The ground produces thorns in general, but it can also produce thorns in particular under the providential judgment of God. It is not that the earth is insufficiently full of resources, it is that the earth is not producing what it is capable of, and worse yet, our natural selfishness ensures that some people over-consume, leaving others without basic necessities. Resources are not fairly distributed, and even when an attempt is made in that direction, inefficiency and corruption often derail the program. Sin, greed, gluttony, and the curse, are all responsible for this state of affairs.

Basically, the Christian is the only person who is in a position to see why the earth has value (it is derivatively good), and why we should take care of it (we were created to do so, and the earth belongs to God). The result should be careful, conscientious, and loving stewardship. Furthermore, the Christian is the only one who can understand why there is both futility in the present order, and bright hope for the future. Currently the world labors under the curse of God for our sin; but when sin has been forever put away, there will be a new heavens and a new earth—the home of ecological righteousness.

2. Sex

I include sex in this discussion because it tends to be a topic which wakes up the bored or distracted reader! So, if you are weary, I expect you to have a renewed attention span at this point. Regrettably, however, your new focus may wear off quickly, because I do not intend to write about sexual intercourse (although this is, undoubtedly, another area in which the gospel saves). Rather—and more profoundly—the gospel saves the sex differentiation between male and female.

Anatomically, males and females are not quite alike. This rather inescapable fact has proven to be the bane of many a radical feminist: no matter how much one says there are no differences between the sexes, such a position is transparently absurd. It is not just a mere distinction in certain organs, either. Men and women are deeply different in a host of biological, psychological, and sociological ways. And, let it be said, if we are true to Darwinism, there is no reason not to use these differences as a basis for discrimination or domination.

Sex differences are beautiful and full of meaning when they are rooted in the creative will of God. Maleness and femaleness are designed and purposeful. Humanness is contained in both equally. That is, in the biblical worldview, both men and women are fully and equally human. Here there is a radical and complete equality. In being equally human, both are equally the image bearers of God.

Yet, in a seeming paradox, these image bearers are also differentiated. There is a special unity, but there is also a powerful diversity. In sexual intercourse (to revive your attention) the two become one. The two are different, yet capable of oneness, only because they are differentiated but equal. In one sense they are not the same, but in another sense they are. In one sense they are fully complete, but in another sense they are incomplete without each other. Adam is the image bearer of God, but it is not good for the man to be without a suitable companion. After all, the God in whose image Adam was made is One God who exists in a Trinitarian relationship. God is One being who is internally differentiated; human beings are one species who are externally differentiated, but capable of becoming mysteriously united into one.

This complementarity saves the whole idea of sex. It saves the value of sex differentiation. It allows us to locate maleness and femaleness in the eternal wise purposes of God. Viewing sex theologically, then, gives us the liberty to embrace, cherish, and rejoice in the fact that God's image bearers are both equal and different. Such an understanding then allows us to make sense of God's directions for how this complementarity is to work out in practice in places, say, like marriage or church. Far from being an accidental and meaningless product of blind chance which limits some and aids others, our sex is an important part of who God made us to be. And when we read that in Christ there is neither male or female, we are brought to recognize that when we are talking about salvation—the most important thing in the world—men and women stand in utter equality. Only this perspective will allow sex distinctions to be properly celebrated and constrained, so that an often contentious issue can be handled redemptively.

3. Worship

As we have seen in previous chapters, sin is a perversion or inversion of proper priorities and perception. God, the only being worthy of praise, is despised, while unworthy substitutes are worshiped in a vain attempt to replace him. As was noted in Romans One, when animals are worshiped instead of the living God, those who are created in the image of their God are reduced to animalistic thought and behavior—and worse. There is no escaping the fact

A Saving Salvation

that human beings were made to worship; they worship God, idols, or themselves. And it is the most glorious or terrifying of truths that we tend to become like that which we worship.

Worshiping anything other than God cannot help but wreak havoc and destruction. The consequences of idolatry sweep over every aspect of our lives. Darkness is confused for light; right is labeled wrong; sin is trumpeted; righteousness is scorned. All the time our "gods" stand by, mute, blind, deaf, and impotent to give counsel or aid. They are not, and cannot be, aware of the fact that they are being worshiped.

When the gospel saves a sinner it takes a person mired in false and misdirected worship and opens their eyes to see the one God who is actually worthy of worship. Since worship is such a massive part of our human experience, this reorientation is nothing short of cataclysmic. The compass we thought pointed due north was actually pointing south by south east. Now that the compass has been reset, accurate navigation through life becomes possible. Our energy, thoughts, actions, speech, and priorities are now properly directed towards God, and the result is that our overall lives chart in the right course.

None of that goes to say that we live perfectly, or that we can attain a type of actualized perfection in our daily lives. What it does mean, however, is that the fundamental orientation of our lives has been corrected and restored. Yes, we go off track and need to make course corrections, but we are at least traveling with a reliable map. Every step takes on new meaning when the ultimate direction changes. Seeing God as God, and being able to love him as oppose to spurn him, results in an entirely different approach to all of life—one in which God receives all the praise and glory.

4. Death

Morbidity is not to be equated with realistically preparing for death. Ignoring death is more morbid than staring it straight in the face. In fact, life cannot be lived until the end of life has found its proper place in our thinking (and feeling). Laughing about death; refusing to talk about death; distracting ourselves so we can't ever think about death—none of this is going to stop death. All human beings will physically die, and with even the most basic application of logical principles, this means that if we are part of the class of human beings, death is something *we* will *personally* experience. Death-in-general will one day become my-death-in-particular. Cosmetic surgery and hair-dye may allow us to convince ourselves that we are a few years further away from death than we really are, but this self-deception is not going to add even a fraction of an hour to our lives. Your friends may think you are 44 instead of 47 (and what could possibly be exciting about that?), but the Grim Reaper is not going to be fooled by appearances. There is a particular and inevitable moment in which every person experiences their own death.

The gospel delivers us from death—and thus from the fear of death which plagues so many people in this life. When we die physically our spirit goes into the presence of the Lord, to await the resurrection when we will receive new and glorified bodies. Death does not usher us into a never ending state of unconsciousness. Death is not the last moment of life, severing us off from all pleasure, joy, love, and meaningful experience. (Although if naturalism is true, one can seriously doubt that there is anything "meaningful" at all, on either side of death.) Death is the last enemy—the last time we fall under the weight of sin's consequences. When we die we are freed from sin and its effects for the rest of time, *provided we are resting in the Christ who defeated death itself in his death on the cross.* As the great theologian John Owen expressed it, there is the Death of Death in the Death of Christ. Jesus defeats death itself for his people, by not allowing death to reign over them or to have the last word. In fact, their physical death becomes the gateway through which they pass to glory. By Christ's power death's consequences are entirely reversed, so that rather than separating us from God forever, through death we are brought into God's very presence. For the redeemed, death has died, and the death of death is life: our life united in Christ's life. The saving gospel saves us from death itself, so that we can truly live life on both sides of our physical death.

Chapter Six

SURVEYING REALITY

God's existence is the first axiom of the Scriptures. He does not exist *as* the universe, nor is the universe co-eternal with him. The universe is something that he summons into existence *ex nihilo*. God exists; the universe does not; then God creates it. The physical universe precedes human life. We discover ourselves to be living in a universe which predates us. Absolutely no human beings observed the very beginning of the space-time universe.

Despite all of our vaunted technological advances, and the hubris associated with "science" in our popular culture, the sheer reality of the matter is that the origins of the universe are shrouded in a virtually impenetrable cloud of mystery (at least today). The hot big bang theory which ruled the field for a few short decades is probably still the reigning paradigm, but various modified oscillating models are still being advanced for consideration. Multi-verses, black holes, vacuums, expansion & contraction, indefinite & infinite inflationary expansion—all such things find their place in cutting edge debates on the origins of the known universe. Such a radical diversity of opinions in the present day should at least raise one cautionary flag—modern scientists know so little about the universe, certainty about the *origins* of the universe is *currently* impossible. It is more or less educated guesswork and speculation. Added to this is the fact that it is rather difficult to know for sure how *unique* the origin of the universe event was, meaning that current observations about how the universe operates today may have nothing to do with how the universe operated in its earliest stages.

There is another alternative for discovering something about the origins of the universe which is open to the human race. We could, as it were, simply ask the One who was there. For the origins of the universe were, as a matter of fact, *observed*; and they were, furthermore, observed by the agent responsible for the event. Now, God has given us a revelation in the Scriptures telling us about the universe's beginning. No, it does not give us all the exhaustive details we would like. ("He also made the stars," as Genesis 1:16c understates. At one level, we would certainly like more information than that!) The creation account does not give us quite the exact time-line that we would like it to provide. It does not go in-depth into chemistry or molecular biology. Yet, what God has told us is sufficient. Once there was no universe; then God willed/spoke it into existence. The universe began to exist; it was purposefully (and intelligently) designed; and it was created for God's glory.

Adam and Eve were charged with subduing the earth, which does not speak of ruthless domination, but intelligent governance and discovery. God made human beings with the capacity to know. Humans can learn, categorize, remember, evaluate, and calculate. Elements from the physical world can be recombined to allow for more precise discovery of other elements in the physical world. (For example, all the material for microscopes is gleaned and refined from the physical world, and such instruments then allow us to learn more about the physical world. It is a spiraling path of greater and deeper discovery.) Our senses are such that we can gain reliable information from our concrete, given physical order. We structure our understanding of the world around us through mental categories, but these mental categories truly do correspond to the reality in which we are situated.

Not only has God located us in a discoverable world—and equipped us to be discoverers of it—he placed us here with himself as a perfectly knowledgeable and reliable guide. God walked and talked with Adam and Eve prior to their fall into sin. The noetic (mentally damaging) effects of sin aside, human beings originally existed in an intimate relationship with an omniscient tutor. As much as God would not constantly "bail out" his young pupils by endlessly supplying answers to their questions when they were perfectly capable of doing some hard work themselves, he was there as an inexhaustible resource. "God, why did you make this like that?" "God, can you help me learn some more about this?" "God, can you please bless my efforts at discovery, for your glory?" Yet—as we have seen—the first humans did not consider God's knowledge and words to be worthwhile. They were content to learn things on their own, forgetting God's wisdom, and even openly opposing his ways.

As a corollary to such open rebellion, God has—like at Babel—often frustrated the idolatrous attempts of human beings to exalt themselves via technology to the heavens. Let us be frank: we are not half as knowledgeable as we think we are. The astonishing rapidity of technological advances in the last century has staggered our collective imaginations. Many grandparents do not understand how to operate the devices that their young grandchildren manipulate with ease. In fact, many grandparents do not even know what such devices *do*. Yet, for the Christian, there is an unsettling counterpart to this advance. True, in a relative sense technology has gone forward by leaps and bounds the last few years, but on the other hand such progress is incredibly *slow*. It has been full of twists, turns, detours, and dead ends. Had we not plunged ourselves into sin, we would be so far ahead in all these areas that today's technological heights would be considered child's play. We would likely be millennia ahead of where we are now—and we would not have done such tremendous harm to our planet, or seen millions starve. The amazing thing is not how much we know; it is how much we do not know, and how many of our received truths are in fact nothing more than misinformation.

As a matter of fact, the very methodologies used by some secular scientists today are *guaranteed* to result in false theories. For example, one of the arguments against intelligent design is that it allows a supernatural designer to be the answer to certain questions. *Science*, so the argument goes, can only deal with physical or natural explanations. If the answer to the question is not physical or natural, it is not scientific. Please do not misunderstand—I am not going to appeal at this point to a "God of the gaps" approach to science. But why should anyone think that every answer to every question must be physical or natural? Why should anyone adopt a method that *rules out* the existence of God, and then goes on to condescendingly report that modern science has not found a need for God? Modern science has not found a need for God because modern science refuses to allow him to exist, even before the first experiment is conducted or the initial observation is made.

Surveying Reality 73

One would have thought that scientists would be open to truth, but the truth is that many scientists are only open to the "natural" order.

This stance, on its own, would not be utterly problematic, if scientists were content to limit the range of their field. Even a Christian scientist can do intensive studies in the natural order, to see the wonderfully intricate material cause and effect universe that God has made. Such a Christian scientist can learn a great deal about the natural order (as much, indeed, as any other scientist), but the Christian scientist has some added advantages. Above all, from a scientific standpoint, the Christian pursues answers to problems, but is not handicapped into simply finding the most probable *naturalistic* explanation. This means that the data does not need to be cut into the Procrustean bed of naturalism. Natural causes are sought, but where they do not exist, the Christian does not have to invent them. By way of contrast, the secularist must chop all data into pieces that fit into a materialistic framework—the data, not the underlying naturalistic framework, is what must be reinterpreted. Over time anomalies build up, and part of the paradigm shifts, but the greater underlying foundation is sacrosanct. Secularists will abandon particular views of the origins of the universe or Darwinism, but they will not, and really cannot, defect from their naturalistic forts.

All of the preceding discussion serves as an introduction to what will follow. The Christian worldview, it will be argued, is necessary for true science. God's existence is necessary as an explanation for the universe's existence (incidentally, he actually is the cause behind it; all other theories are simply wrong!). Furthermore, God's existence is necessary for humans to have warranted knowledge, or true justified belief (I am purposefully not being picky or precise here on terminology—my apologies to the philosophers or epistemologists in the reading audience.) In fact, the Christian worldview alone can defend the Christian worldview. Beyond this, even the principles of the Christian worldview must be used by the *secularists* in order to defend their own system. Since this is the case, the very fact that the secularist attempts to do science or defend their worldview is a proof that their worldview is false. In other words, the secularists must *rely on* precisely what they *deny* in order to even argue for their view! Hopefully this point will be clarified in the following chapters.

At this juncture it may be useful to present a framework for defending the Christian faith. Apologists defend the faith. Given the nature of this task, apologists must first understand the faith they seek to defend. Apologetics does not start with philosophy—it starts with theology. For the defender of the faith must be acquainted with the distinctive doctrines of the faith. In fact, the task of the apologist is not so much to establish the existence of some kind of supreme being as it is to defend the doctrinal truths which are particular to Christianity. We are to give an answer to everyone who asks us (cf., I Peter 3:15), but in context the questioner is asking about "the hope that is within you." If I may be very bold, it would seem to be that the answer to this question about why we have hope is not rooted in a philosophical argument—it is rooted in the work and person of the Lord Jesus Christ. The reason why I have hope within me (regardless of persecution and unjustly suffering *for being righteous*, which is the greater context in I Peter) is because I have been regenerated, my sins have been completely atoned for by the glorious substitutionary death of Jesus Christ, God is propitiated, my faith is a sign of my inclusion in the Lord's new covenant people, I will never be left or forsaken, and my eternal future is assured to be with the Lamb in sinless and consummated perfection. So, if you are asking me why I can have hope even when you are persecuting me, that's the short-list!

If we are to equip the church to defend or save the saving gospel, the gospel itself must first be understood. The church must simply have better theology. The Bible must be learned, in both its over-arching plot, and in its small, "verse" size bites. What are needed today are more knowledge of Scripture, more godly character, and more prayer. Apologists must be steeped in the Bible. Appealing to Scripture is the best way to provide an answer to a question. Someone may reject the authority of the Bible, but that is not our business. The Bible is God's special revelation; it is inerrant, infallible, and authoritative. People may reject God's word the way Adam and Eve did—but that is a rather poor example to follow. The people of God must consistently, comfortably, and humbly rest in the Scriptures. Again, if you are asked to provide a reason for the hope that is within you, and you do *not* use the Bible in your answer, I think you have failed, because the reason for our hope is *only found in the pages of God's Word*.

"Ah," comes the reply, "but this is circular reasoning. You use the Bible to prove the Bible. Your hope is grounded in a book that tells you about your hope. I, of course, cannot accept this line of thinking." Such a common reply rests on two fundamental misunderstandings.

In the first place, all appeals to an ultimate standard or authority must terminate in that authority's authority. The Bible, as the Word of God, is fully authoritative. What it says is to be accepted as true. Since the Bible makes claims about itself, these claims *ultimately* have their authority in their own self-authentication. Unlike Adam and Eve, we do not need to inquire as to whether or not what God has said is true. Anything God says is true by definition. Neither is this any more circular than appeals to other standards of authority. One person says they only follow the dictates of rationality. Why do they say this? Well, because it seems *reasonable* to appeal to *reason*. This is circular. Using your reason to appeal to the standard of your reason is circular reasoning. Others claim to follow logic—because, naturally, it seems *logical* to do so. Still others will only rely on their senses (which is incredibly philosophically naïve), because, after all, their senses are reliable. So they ground their authority in their senses on the fact that they rely on their senses. Perhaps the reader can see the circle there on their own.

Having said all this, however, it is also true that such circles are usually not so crassly stated. In practice, whatever the theory, we tend to ground ultimate authority not so much on a vicious circle as on an ever increasing spiral of knowledge. For the Christian, as the Holy Spirit works in them to understand the Scriptures, the ultimate authority of the Bible is found in God's Word, but the worldview of the Scriptures also can be exhaustively applied to the real world that we find ourselves in. This, of course, is not surprising. When we stand on the authority of the Bible, and then seek to apply God's truth to God's creation, we discover that the worldview of the Bible allows us to understand and accurately interpret our lives and the universe. By way of contrast, the secularist or, say, pantheist worldviews, when applied to real life, fail to provide grounds for meaningful interpretation. The worldview of materialism simply fails on its own terms. Every worldview, besides the biblical one, is ultimately insufficient.

In the second place, the biblical worldview is also buttressed and supported by secondary or collaborating sources. While the ultimate authority of the Bible is to be found in the fact that it is God's Word, data gleaned from all sorts of resources fits into, and confirms, the validity of the biblical teachings. Strictly speaking, such secondary confirmation is not necessary—but it is what we would expect, given the worldview contained in the Scriptures. Although the disciplines of archaeology, history, science, and philosophy are not ultimately authoritative, the findings in each of these fields of study do lend considerable support to the Bible. Now, the putative facts (which are really interpretations) of the cult of scientism do not fit with the worldview of the Bible, but this should cause nobody (except the priests of scientism) any alarm. (*Scientism* says that if something cannot be found using the scientific method, it does not exist. Many modern atheists fall into this camp.) Historical documents, archaeological discoveries, scientific data, and philosophical arguments (which rely heavily on logic and reason) align themselves with God's truth. God's Word is truth—and this is seen to be true time and again. I believe my wife loves me because she tells me that she does; and her love is proved hundreds of times every day. I believe the truth of the Bible because God says so; and his Word is seen to be true every day and in every discipline.

Chapter Seven

GOD'S CREATED ORDER

In the beginning of the last chapter we noted that a fully agreed upon, modern day scientific explanation of the origin of the universe does not, in fact, actually exist. There is no agreed upon explanation. On the contrary, there are multiple theories in competition with one another, and a great deal of speculation. There is a plethora of: "*If* this was like that, then *maybe* this happened." Some argue that there is no known natural explanation for the existence of the known universe—so of course its existence is dependent on *unknown* universes we have not yet discovered. (This, let it be said, is not very good science; but it is a required conclusion for scientism.) Much of this dissonance is understandable, given how little we know about the beginning of our universe. Furthermore, all calculations and theories must *assume* (not prove!) that there is a certain uniformity to the way things are now working in the universe, and the way they have worked in the past. This assumption is not grounded in observation (nor can it be). It is simply assumed because it has to be assumed. Yet, if the origin of the universe is entirely a unique event, it is severely begging the question just to assume that we can accurately determine how things unfolded back then given our observations over the past few years.

Still, if there has been a theory that has won widespread support over the last several decades, it is the big bang theory. I believe that there is a good argument which, taking the premises of the big bang theory, indicates that there would have to be a cause behind it. The point is not that the universe is billions of years old: the point is that if the universe began to exist at *any* time, it required a cause. In my judgment, this argument is quite good. However, I do not believe that it should be relied on entirely to prove the existence of God. In part this is due to the fact that, with so little known about the origins of the universe, it is entirely plausible to suspect that five decades from now (or even five years from now) science will be trumpeting a completely different theory for the origins of the universe. It is far better to rely on the Bible's account than the shifting sands of scientific theorizing. The argument I am about to unpack—regardless of the big bang theory—does fit well into the biblical teaching of creation *ex nihilo*. (As a matter of fact, this argument was advanced many centuries before the big bang theory was even postulated.)

In the present day, the apologist most active in propagating and defending this particular argument is William Lane Craig. The name of the argument is the *Kalam Cosmological Argument*. Craig relies heavily on big bang theory calculations, and the testimony of the greater scientific community, but the foundational points can be abstracted out of his particular approach. The main point is that scientists argue that the universe came into existence *out of nothing*, but this is rather absurd. If the universe came into existence out of nothing, it is an effect—and analytically, an effect requires a cause.

Craig outlines his argument very clearly:

1. Whatever begins to exist has a cause.
2. The universe began to exist.

3. Therefore, the universe has a cause.[4]

This is a deductively valid syllogism, which means that if premises 1 and 2 are true, the conclusion must be true (i.e., sound) as well. The first premise (Whatever begins to exist has a cause) seems to be virtually self-evident. If something comes into existence or begins to exist, this would require a cause. The only alternative is that something literally came from nothing. So you have nothing—not a principle, energy, law, material or anything at all—and from this nothing emerges something (like, say, a universe). Such a line of thinking seems to border on preposterous. Nothing does not produce something. Something does not come from nothing. If something comes into existence, its very existence proves that there was some-other-thing that caused it. It is entirely *unreasonable* to argue that something comes from nothing.

The second premise (The universe began to exist) has enjoyed a great consensus of scientific scholarship for a number of decades. So, if someone denies this point, they are at least rejecting the common opinion of the scientific community. Since secularists are currently having a torrid love affair with scientism, denying this premise is more than a little inconsistent. Future calculations may cause modification to the accepted wisdom of this premise, but for the last

---

[4] William Lane Craig, *Reasonable Faith: Christian Truth and Apologetics, Revised* (Wheaton: Crossway Books, 1994), 92. Craig's elaboration and defense of these points is found on p. 92-125. Craig engages Stephen Hawking, scientists, philosophers, and other explanations of the universe's origins in these pages. The diligent reader should consult him. My aims at the present are much more modest and general.

few decades, scientists have argued that the universe did indeed begin to exist.

Where does this leave us? Well, it seems rather obvious to most people that since something cannot come from nothing, if something begins to exist it requires an antecedent cause. And, since science has taught that the universe did in fact begin to exist, one would think that scientists would be quick to start searching for the cause of the universe. Strangely, this has not been done with the vigor one would have expected. In fact, many individuals have just said that we have to chalk up the existence of our universe to chance. It didn't exist; now it does; it wasn't caused; it came from nothing. God was not the cause, because God does not exist. Science can account for everything without appealing to the supernatural!

It is at this point where the blinders are obvious to anyone who is not wearing them. God would seem to make a rather splendid causal agent for the existence of the universe. In fact, the Bible teaches that God did pre-exist the universe, and he did bring the universe into existence out of nothing other than his own will and power. Then, millennia later, scientists say they have discovered that the universe began to exist out of nothing. This was known by God's people for thousands of years: ironically, science has lagged behind the times.

"Now," some will retort, "if everything needs an antecedent cause to account for its existence, what accounts for God's existence"? Such an objection rests on a simple misunderstanding—one which Bertrand Russell never figured out. Whatever *begins* to exist requires a cause—not *whatever* exists. This is why philosophers have made arguments to a First Cause. Not everything can come from an antecedent cause, or you would have an impossible infinite regress. This means that each cause would need a cause: but at some point you just need a cause that is uncaused. You can no more count an infinite sequence into the past than you can successively count up from 1 to the end of infinity. Try it, if you disagree. Let me know when you reach the end. 1, 2, 3, etc. -1, -2, -3, etc. You cannot reach the end of an infinite sequence by successive addition, whether you are counting forwards or backwards. This is why you cannot have an infinite regress of causes, and also why the universe cannot be eternal. (The universe cannot be eternal because if you take a whole unit of measurement like a second, you cannot start at the present "0 seconds" and count back to the beginning of the supposedly infinite number of seconds. If you cannot reach the beginning from the present by adding one second to another, you cannot reach the present from the beginning either! Reversing the direction you are traversing does not make the impossible possible.)

If something comes into existence, it must come from something. God is eternal and self-sufficient, and therefore does not begin to exist. He naturally and essentially exists. Clearly something exists as opposed to nothing (the reader, for example, exists). So there really is a reality; things actually do exist. They either come into existence out of nothing, or they (or their cause) have existed eternally. The universe has not existed *eternally*, but the universe does exist. So we are left asking the question: What eternally existing cause can account for the existence of the universe? And we are left with the Bible's answer: God, the self-existent, eternal creator, is the cause.

This answer is, of course, denied by many. Some will say that the universe did just come from nothing, and that's that. Others will argue that the existence of the universe is so anomalous that nothing known from our observations *in* the universe can be applied to its beginning (i.e., we observe cause and effect *in* the universe as it is now, but this does not mean there was cause and effect *for* the universe). More will simply assert that the big bang model is wrong, and further scientific studies will overturn it, leaving the universe as an eternal entity. Still others will concede that the universe is an effect that requires a cause, but this cause need only be finite since the universe is only finite, and a cause only needs to be sufficient to produce its effect. In other words, it is illegitimate to postulate an unobserved cause which is many orders of magnitude greater than the observed effect. My opinion is not that the *kalam* cosmological argument *proves* the existence of God, but rather that it serves as a confirmation to what believers already *know* to be true from the Scriptures. We can, of course, be as nitpicky as we like when it comes to logic, but it is hard to deny that if the universe requires a cause, God would definitely be a great candidate for that role.

In the biblical account of creation, not only does God bring the world into existence out of nothing, he also carefully crafts the earth and provides a suitable environment for all kinds of flora and fauna. One creature on earth represents the pinnacle of God's work: human beings are created as the special image bearers of God. They are rational, relational, aesthetic, moral agents. God made a home for them, and modern science is helping us to understand just how complicated and precise our home had to be in order for us to survive.

God's Created Order

There are so many factors making our existence possible that it is literally beyond the scope of human comprehension. We can record the odds, but the numbers are so huge they are basically meaningless to us. The odds against the universe being able to support human life are astronomical for hundreds of individual factors, all of which must be perfect for us to exist in the first place.

For example:

1. If the rate of the universe's expansion was one-millionth slower, the earth would be thousands and thousands of degrees hotter. The whole universe must have been moving at precisely this speed or we could never have begun to exist. That means that from the beginning, if the universe was expanding at one million km/hour, and we slowed the speed by one km/hour, we would die. Lucky for us!

2. The size of the earth, the tilt of its axis, the speed of its rotation, the amount of water on it, the activity of its tectonic plates, and more all have to be balanced on a razor's edge for human life to even be possible. The sun needs to be just the size, distance, temperature, and age that it is for human life to exist. The moon needs to be exactly where it is too, or earth would be uninhabitable. Change any of these factors by a few percentage points, and the earth becomes absolutely desolate. This, of course, is to say nothing of the chemical composition of the atmosphere.

3. In the end, there are dozens of constants and requirements that need to be perfect for human life to exist. For them all to work together, the odds are over trillions and trillions to one. In fact, "trillion" is simply the wrong word to use. We have no capacity to grasp the size of the actual

figure! From the moment of the creation of the universe, down to the arrangement and constitution of the earth, if things changed by one part in a thousand for some factors, one part in a million for others, or one part in a billion for others, there would be no possibility of human life.

Look it up: the data is not questioned, it is the interpretation of the data that is questioned. Atheists say that all this happened by chance. Christians (and many non-Christian philosophers and scientists) say the universe exhibits clear evidence of design. The issue is this: the universe could have been different than it is in trillions of ways, and human life would have been literally impossible. Or, the universe could have been *exactly* the way it is, and human life was not only a possibility, but actually came to be. If you were blindfolded and had to pick one blue button out of trillions and trillions and trillions of red buttons, what would you think of the odds?

For the atheist, the argument is that the universe came from nothing. What came from nothing happened to be the one in a trillion trillion universes that did not make human life absolutely impossible right from the start. And then, later on, human life actually did come into existence (we have not, of course, even touched on the odds against evolution, which even evolutionists find fantastically improbable).

Let us pretend that there is a button making machine. It makes one billion different sizes of buttons. It also paints each button one particular color out of ten trillion possible colors. Furthermore, it produces one hundred million various shapes. Now, you have a coat that is missing a button. The button machine produces each button in a completely random manner, but only one combination of size, color, and shape will match your coat. The button machine cranks up, and the right size randomly pops up! Then, the right color, (#4, 109, 985, 869, 435—kind of an aqua blue) just happens to accidentally be selected. Then, out of one hundred million various shapes, the perfect shape randomly is picked. Of course, in an atheist universe, there is one other factor: *there is no button making machine.* The perfect button just happened to pop into existence out of nothing.

Now, the objection will come that we are getting the order backwards. There is no suit for the button making machine to line up with. Whatever button is produced will be the right "fit" because the suit is built around the button, not the button for a pre-existing suit. This objection is not, however, very compelling. Let's just change the details from buttons to universes capable of (accidentally and randomly!) producing self-conscious, sentient, self-reflective creatures. There are virtually an infinite number of universes which are not sustainable, which are totally chaotic, which are far too hot, or random, or lawless, or whatever. Some do not contain the hydrogen atom. Others do not have carbon. Some have a law of gravity that is 10 times stronger than the force of gravity across our universe. Still others have too much dark matter. We could, of course, go on this way indefinitely. The point is that in every one of these alternate universes the conditions do not obtain for the production of sentient life. That is, in every one of these universes, nothing knows that the universe even exists. Yet here we are, in a universe which supposedly came from nothing, and we are self-consciously thinking away. Thankfully, the universe which came from nothing was the one out of the trillions of possibilities which could produce self-reflective thinkers and observers!

When something comes into existence out of nothing (which is impossible, anyway) it does not have to conform to any guidelines. The question is not just: "Why is gravity just the way it happens to be?" the question is: "Why does gravity even exist in the first place?" You see, gravitational forces have to be exactly perfect all through the universe in order for humans to exist, and although there is no reason for it to be perfectly tuned for human existence, there is also no reason for gravity to even exist, period. When something pops into existence out of nothing, it is difficult to see why it must contain the law of gravity! Why did the perfect amount of matter and chemicals appear? Why did the perfect explosion set a perfect trajectory for the perfect formation of a perfect environment for human life? According to atheists, the answer is sheer dumb luck. According to the Bible, the story is that the universe was created by an omniscient being who designed it for human life. Which of these seems more rational?

It is no good to say, as some atheists do, that the universe had to be some way, and this is just the way it happened to be. The point is that this universe is the home of sentient, self-conscious thinkers, who are able to study this universe in a rational way. The universe could have been trillions and trillions of different ways, and there would be no self-conscious thinkers. Yet here we are, thinking away, and no betting man in the world could believe this came about by chance. The odds of a universe having the necessary makeup to produce and support human life are far smaller than we can comprehend. The odds of a universe coming into existence out of nothing are literally zero.

Could something come from nothing, and through blind chance create life from non-living matter? Could this life then somehow become self-conscious? Could this self-conscious life just somehow then become *moral*? No. We know that God created the universe and human beings because of the teachings of the Scriptures, but science, reason, and logic help to reveal how wonderfully fantastic this creation is.

Chapter Eight

THE EVIL IN THE ORDER

Granting for argument's sake that the universe is created by God, the question then becomes: If God is omnipotent, omniscient, and perfectly good, why is there evil in the universe? Generally, the two horns of the problem are supposed to be that if God is omnipotent he would have the power to keep sin out of his creation, and if he were all good he would exercise that power. Thus, if God had these attributes (as Christians say he does) then evil would not exist. So, either God is all-good but not all-powerful, or *vice versa*. How should a Christian respond to this charge?

Although there are many different responses that can be given, since this is not a work of academic philosophy we will try to stick to the main point. All we need to do is add one more premise to the equation:

1. God is omnipotent, omniscient (i.e., he infallibly knows everything that has happened in the past, everything happening now, everything that will happen in the future, and everything that could even possibly have happened but did not), and perfectly good.

2. God created a good world *ex nihilo*, but now there is evil in the universe.

3. God has a morally excellent and sufficient reason for allowing evil to exist.

Now, it is important to notice that this piece of reasoning contains not a whiff of logical contradiction. In fact, it is commonly recognized today by both atheist and theist philosophers alike that the existence of God and the existence of evil are not—strictly speaking—logically contradictory. Anyone who claims that God *cannot* exist because evil exists is just simply uninformed. They need to read more modern atheist philosophers!

Recognizing that the originally posed problem failed, atheists have resorted to another approach. The main contention is not that the existence of God and the existence of evil are logically contradictory, but rather that the existence of evil is *not what we would expect* given the existence of God. In other words, the problem is not one of strict logical deduction, but one of evidential or probabilistic induction. Surely it is surprising, according to this line of reasoning, to have God create a world that contains such a large array of deep and pointless suffering.

For starters, it is very difficult to establish that there really is such a thing as *pointless* (i.e., gratuitous) suffering. That there is pointless suffering cannot just be asserted as if it were a self-evident truth. In order to demonstrate that there really is such a thing as pointless suffering, the objector needs to point (pardon the pun) to a real example of pointless suffering. To establish the truth of their claim that such a real life example is genuinely pointless, they will have to prove that there is no point to it *at all*. They will have to prove that the instance of evil in question did not produce a greater good in the future, or that it did not come from a good principle in the past.

This last sentence needs some explanation. Generally speaking, systems of ethics can be divided up into consequential and non-consequential theories. For a consequen-

The Evil in the Order

tialist, something is good if it produces an effect in which the good outweighs the bad. For a non-consequentialist, something is good if it is intrinsically good (e.g., telling the truth is good, not because it produces good effects, but because honesty is a virtue by itself). Our objector then has to: 1. Identify an example of pointless evil; 2. Explain how it could not produce a greater good in the future; *or* 3. Explain how it did not come from something good in itself. (The most common defense for 3 is that God made human beings as free moral agents, which is a very great, intrinsic good. If we abuse our moral freedom by committing evil, the consequences of our actions do not override the fact that it was good for God to make us as free moral beings capable of significant moral choices which could either help or harm others.)

Either way, the objector now needs to appeal to omniscience to establish their charge with any force. They need to know everything in order to know *for sure* that the case of pointless evil they identified is truly pointless. Unless they know how their particular case fits into or affects the past, present, or future, they cannot claim to know that it is pointless. It is no argument for someone to say that God cannot exist because *they* cannot see what point a particular instance of suffering might possibly have. God simply does not have the responsibility to sit down with each one of us and explain why he allowed every single instance of evil to occur. Furthermore, it is a touch arrogant for us to even think we could comprehend every detail of God's eternally wise plan were he to reveal it to us. Perhaps it is more likely that my two year old daughter could complete a Ph.D. in physics before going to kindergarten. There are some realities which are simply beyond the scope of our limited and finite intellects. But since God is omniscient we at least know that *he* knows; and since he is all-good we know that he has a morally acceptable reason. We are now in a position to re-frame the problem:

1. God is omnipotent, etc.
2. Evil exists.
3. Since God exists, there is no such thing as a genuine case of pointless suffering.

Even if there is no logically compelling reason to think that there is any pointless evil given the existence of God, the evidential argument is still not entirely overthrown. After all, pointless suffering or evil is not a necessary part of it. The objector has every right to reply that he cannot possibly prove the existence of pointless suffering, but that the existence of evil and suffering are still not what we would expect to find given the existence of God. How much weight does this argument carry?

The amount of credence given to this argument (as is the case with any argument about the existence of God) entirely depends on how the particular argument is supposed to function in a larger scheme of investigation. For example, if somebody came to believe in the existence of God by studying the cosmological argument, and they came to be convinced that God existed, it is unlikely that the evidence from evil would carry too much weight. After all, a God who can create the universe might be apt to do some surprising things! Even though some of what God allows may be counterintuitive to us, why should we think that our intuitions and preferences are an accurate gauge of what God would/should do? On the other hand, if somebody began their thinking about God with the argument from evil, they

The Evil in the Order

may well think that their first step into the investigation had turned up evidence which seems to count more against God's existence than for it.

As Romans One makes clear, however, human beings are not cut adrift in nature, with God expecting them to construct a philosophical case that comes out with more weight in the "God exists" side of the ledger. If he did, all we could have is proportional belief (e.g., I take it, on the evidence, that I am justified to belief with 76% of myself that God more likely than not exists). Paul's argument in Romans was that every human being knows God already. The problem is not that they need to employ logic to find God; the problem is they use "logic" to avoid admitting that God is real. Atheism is an attempt to rationally justify what one knows deep down to be utterly false.

The problem of evil, interestingly enough, is actually a bigger problem for the atheist than for the believer. This is owing to numerous factors, one of which is the inescapable reality that unbelievers cannot explain where morals come from. Precisely where and when did morals emerge in an amoral, chance universe that blindly and accidentally formed creatures from amoral forces and material? Surely the very notions of right and wrong are flagrant category mistakes for such a world! Morality is nothing other than the emotional preferences of cosmic accidents (and how widely their preferences vary!). Right and wrong, good and evil, are ultimately rooted in nothingness. Why should anyone take human morality seriously, or even think that human thinking about morality has any bearing on what is really right or wrong at all? Either way there is no real morality, and neither is there any reason to think that if there were, evolved accidents would be very trustworthy or accurate in their moral perceptions.

What does all this mean? Well, it just means that on the basis of the amoral, chance universe posited by atheists, there is no reason to suspect that the idea of human morality is even coherent. If it is not coherent or meaningful, *why is it so devastating to attack God with it?* The unbeliever says God does not exist because of the evil found in the world. But the unbeliever cannot even begin to give a cogent reason for believing in morality in the first place. So, they use something that they cannot explain and which cannot even exist in their worldview (the category of evil) to argue that God does not exist. The atheist has to rely on the principles of the biblical worldview to even make this case. All they can say is that there is no real evil in their worldview, but in the biblical one suffering creates a problem—but this is untrue. In the biblical worldview the believer submits to the greater goodness and wisdom of the Lord who has a morally sufficient reason—fully known to him—why he created a world which became tainted by sin.

There is another side to this discussion, too. According to the biblical worldview, the question is wrongly focused. Rather than wondering why there is so much suffering in the world, one is left to wonder why there is so much pleasure, happiness, contentment, and joy. Given the fact that God hates sin, and given the fact that we are all sinners deserving death and hell, it is an astounding testimony to God's rich grace that we consider suffering to be so abnormal and strange. The very fact that some people can complain about how hard life is testifies to the greater fact that their lives are not nearly as hard as they should be. They

The Evil in the Order

are upheld and sustained by God's gracious and powerful hand, and even while they grumble they only do so because God in mercy has withheld from them their just due. That this world is not as bad as hell itself is only because God has not immediately punished everyone as their sins deserve.

Taking the Christian story at face value, then, dissolves the problem of suffering and evil that we find on planet earth here and now. But another question knocks the inquiry back a step: Where exactly did evil come from in the first place? This is a question atheists cannot answer, but it is one that Christians need to wrestle with. Why did God allow evil to exist at all? Why did he not just forbid its existence? Why did he create this world, knowing as he did that it would bring sin, rebellion, and the curse into existence?

Again, the only answer required is that although we do not know God's exhaustive counsel, we do know that he must have a good reason for creating this world, even though it would fall into sin. I think that perhaps the following preliminary sketch may be along the right lines. The greatest good is to bring glory to God, because he is worthy of being recognized and appreciated as the maximally excellent being. There is no greater being, *nor could there be*. God exists in perfect, personal, internal harmony, one essence in three persons. It was his good pleasure to create other beings—dependent and derivative beings—who could exist in such a way as to benefit from the maximum perfections of God. Being finite, such creatures could not comprehend God in the totality of his being, but had to learn about him in true but partial ways. Rather than fully knowing the God Who Is, they had to learn that God is holy, just, etc., building up categories of understanding the divine nature.

To reveal his nature and character in its fullest way to finite creatures, God designed a universe and a plan which would demonstrate the various aspects—as we perceive them—of his being. The love of God could best be displayed to creatures by the self-sacrifice of Jesus Christ for the ugly and "unlovable." While this may not be the best way of understanding this, the main point is that the cross is the highest revelation of the character and attributes of God in the history of the world. In order to have this revelation, it was necessary for there to be death; and in order to have death, there had to be sin. Creation history runs to the cross. God receives maximal glory in the willing, substitutionary death of Jesus Christ. Calvary was not an afterthought—it was the main point.

From the eternal wise counsel of the Godhead the creation, fall, and redemption were planned. At not one single moment does God fail to operate the universe with full, sovereign control. The creation decree of God included all that will happen. Yet, human beings are fully responsible for what they do. This may be hard to understand, but it is certainly not incoherent.

Philosophers debate whether or not human beings have free will, or if their every act and thought is determined. Genetics can be determinative for certain things, as can environment. Certainly, just being human creatures limits our range of options (e.g., I am not free to choose to flap my arms and fly). Non-determinists argue that human beings really are free. In philosophical literature, even this free-

The Evil in the Order

dom is very small and truncated. It is also true that philosophers who believe in genuine free will seem to be a minority. Yes, we tend to naturally *suppose* that we are free to make decisions; but upon rigorous reflection, it seems like this is more of an illusion than a fact.

Thankfully, the Bible takes a stance on the issue of freedom and determinism. And it concludes—as do many top philosophers—that we can be significantly free and responsible even though our actions are at the same time guaranteed to only be performed one way. When I willingly do something—whether or not I could have avoided doing it is irrelevant—I am morally responsible for the action. This stance (oh so painfully oversimplified in just two paragraphs!) is referred to as *compatibilism*. Freedom and responsibility is *compatible* with some forms of determinism.

(A note for the philosophically minded: I am here adopting what is sometimes called "soft compatibilism." It represents a rejection of the libertarian "forking garden paths" model of free possibility, as well as a basic acceptance of Frankfurt-examples.)

Certainly this concept can be fleshed out at great length and with appropriate rigor. At this point, however, it may be best to quickly survey some biblical texts that clearly teach the overriding sovereignty of God and the full responsibility of human agents. Much, much more could be said at each point, but the case is not too difficult to comprehend in its main contour. Peripheral details will be studiously avoided so that the central truth can be seen without distraction.

First, the position I am advocating here can be nicely illustrated with the story of Joseph in Genesis 37-50. As most readers undoubtedly know, Joseph's brothers plotted to kill him (37:18), but instead they sold him into slavery (v. 26-28). Through a tumultuous ordeal, Joseph winds up being thrown into a dungeon prison for having the integrity not to sleep with his master's wife, who then lies about him out of spite. Even in prison, however, the Lord was with Joseph, and blessed him (39:23). Eventually, through the God-given ability to interpret dreams, Joseph is taken out of prison and placed in the court of Pharaoh. He is given the insight to know that God is sending a great famine to the land of Egypt, and so he is placed in charge of preparing the reserves of food for that time.

As the famine grinds on year after year, Joseph's brothers are forced to make the journey to Egypt to buy food. Through a fascinating sequence of twists and turns, Joseph ends up revealing his identity to his brothers. Notice what he says (added emphasis is mine to highlight the brothers' responsibility and God's sovereignty):

> Then Joseph said to his brothers: "Come close to me." When they had done so, he said, "I am your brother Joseph, the one *you sold* into Egypt! And now, do not be distressed and do not be angry with yourselves for selling me here, because it was to save lives that *God sent me* ahead of you. For two years now there has been famine in the land, and for the next five years there will not be plowing and reaping. But *God sent me* ahead of you to preserve you a remnant on earth and to save your lives by a great deliverance" (Gen. 45:4-7).

Notice that Joseph states very clearly that his brothers *sold him*, but it was actually *God who sent him*. The brothers sold him out of hatred and jealousy; God sent him to save many

The Evil in the Order

lives—including the lives of his brothers! Were the brothers not responsible for selling Joseph? Of course they were. Was God in sovereign control over the sale of Joseph into slavery? Of course he was. Both are true simultaneously.

This interpretation is made even more plain in Genesis 50:20, where Joseph says to his brothers: "You intended to harm me, but God intended it for good to accomplish what is now being done, the saving of many lives." Here it is clear that the brothers sold Joseph out of *evil motives*, but God sent Joseph *to do good*. The same event—the sale of Joseph into slavery—is done by sinful beings in a sinful way, but also by a good God to produce good. Certainly Joseph did not see the end when he was sold, nor did he see what good would come when he was thrown into jail for doing the right thing. Neither do we need to know everything, nor do we need to see what good might come from evil, in order to trust in God's ways.

The second illustration comes from the New Testament. In Acts 4:23-31, the early church is praying in the face of persecution and imprisonment. As they reflect on the Psalms that teach that the world unsuccessfully rages against God, they acknowledge that Herod and Pilate and all the enemies of Christ, when they crucified Jesus: "did what your [God's] power and will had decided beforehand should happen," (v. 28). Did this mean that the enemies of Christ were not morally responsible for what they did? On the contrary, during Peter's sermon at Pentecost he emphatically stated: "This man [Jesus] was handed over to you by God's set purpose and foreknowledge; and you, with the help of wicked men, put him to death by nailing him to the cross," (Acts 2:24).

It is easy to blunt the thrust of Peter's words, but the fact remains that the crucifixion was *completely determined by God*, and yet those who nailed Jesus to the cross did so out of hatred and their desire to murder him. In fact, they were acting as the ultimate rebels and haters of God; but all they could do was fulfill God's set purpose and foreknowledge—that which his will and power had decided *beforehand* would happen.

Just like with Joseph (but in a higher way) we see here that the Bible teaches that wicked people do wicked things for which they are fully responsible. Yet, at the same time, God is directing and guiding all things according to his will, purpose, and plan. Sinners are responsible for their sin, not God. But God is in control even over the sinful things that happen. Sinners act out of wicked motives, but God always acts for the greatest good imaginable, which is his own honor, praise, and glory. Thus the same event is morally good or bad depending in part on intentionality. (There is no time to really pick up this theme now. Read Isaiah 10 and I Corinthians 13 for a jumping off point into the relationship between human motives and acts, morality, evil, good, and God's intentions and purposes.)

Has it ever occurred to you that Calvinists and Arminians, at least at the local church level, seem to have half a dozen or so proof-texts for their position, which they just quote past each other? Some texts speak of God being in control of all things, while others speak of human responsibility ("free will" as a concept must be read into these texts, since the phrase "free will" does not appear in them). The inference is that if humans are responsible then God cannot be in ultimate control of their actions. This inference is simply false. In fact, the Bible does contain texts which highlight the responsibility humans bear for their decisions and deeds. It also, of course, contains texts which clearly teach that God is in comprehensive, sovereign control of all things. The *problem* is not in the Bible. The *problem* is introduced when people fail to grasp the truth that *God's sovereignty and human responsibility are fully compatible*. It is wrong-headed and methodologically disastrous to start reading the Bible after one has already decided what conditions must be satisfied in order for a person to be free, or for an act to be loving. Rather, we should come to the Scriptures to see how God understands and defines such things as freedom, moral responsibility, and love. According to God's own word, libertarian free will is not necessary for genuine freedom. Furthermore, he is in control of everything that happens, including the free acts of rational moral agents. Yet, the responsibility for sin is with the immediate cause (i.e., the acting agent). God never has, never will, and never can sin.

Let me be frank: if you can't understand any of this, just make sure you are clear on the following points.

1. God is not evil, nor has he ever done anything evil.

2. Human beings are morally responsible beings who are responsible for what they do.

3. God is sovereign over all things.

4. God knows *precisely* how all this works out—and that is all we are required to know.

We should be humble around these issues. There are very great mysteries here, and although we can scratch the surface of them, we are just not equipped to probe them to a great depth. Like with every other study of God and his ways, it seems that we very quickly run into a brick wall where our knowledge stops, and we are left to humbly adore the God who is infinitely greater in love, knowledge, wisdom and power than we are. A compatibilistic view of the will may never be adequately formulated by us, but it is the view which is taught in God's word. Hence it is true; no matter how far (or short) our articulation of the concept can take us.

Where does this leave us when it comes to the problem of evil, then? Well, evil is part of the plan of God. We are immediately responsible for the evil that we do, and are guilty. God is in sovereign control over all things, but sinlessly so. We act in accordance with God's eternal, sovereign plan, yet our free agency is not illusory. God is not the doer of evil, but evil is a component of his overarching plan to bring himself glory which he richly deserves. The rebellious sinner desperately wants to be autonomous, and so hates the sovereign God. The Christian has been restored to moral sanity, and so falls down to worship the incomprehensible majesty of God. Such a believing response is just part of the journey, where God's redeemed and regenerate people learn to live with faith, seeking greater understanding.

Chapter Nine

THE RESURRECTION

Historical arguments do not prove the truth of the resurrection. This should not be too defeating, since historical arguments are really quite limited in what they can prove, depending on how skeptical one decides one wants to be. Jesus' followers do not need to present an argument which proves that he rose from the dead: Jesus himself already presented this argument by appearing to his followers in his post-resurrection state. They were then responsible for telling others what had happened. Inspired by the Holy Spirit, the resurrection account and appearances have been recorded, so these constitute all the proof the Christian needs to embrace the event as factual. Still, like in so many other areas, the resurrection makes sense out of the data of history and the deliverances of reason.

In order to have a really first-rate resurrection, you need to have a dead body. Death is a necessary, but not a sufficient, condition for a resurrection to occur. Although you certainly need more than just a dead body in order to have a resurrection, you cannot get away with less than that! The Bible contains many references to the crucifixion of Jesus. Other references are found in non-Christian historical records and sources from the first century. That Jesus lived and died by crucifixion is simply not doubted by serious historians today who have studied ancient history.

The case for the resurrection of Jesus is quite often made, and even when it is presented in nuanced ways the core of the case does not vary widely. I will present a sketch of the normal argument, and then identify some of the limits which it must live with. Just before proceeding this way, however, one very short digression is in order.

There is a long case which can be made for the historical accuracy, reliability, and purity of the biblical manuscripts which are extant. Textual critics of the Bible are overwhelmed with the raw number of early copies of the texts, particularly with the New Testament. The copies of the texts are very early and exceptionally accurate. Due to the quick dispersion of the manuscripts, the fidelity of the copying practices, and the sheer number of copies, scholars can know the exact content of the original writings with a degree of certainty of *over* 99%. Furthermore, where there are discrepancies and uncertainties remaining, not a single major teaching of Christianity is involved. The very minute number of places where uncertainty remains is therefore largely inconsequential. For more on the purity, reliability, and transmission of the texts, scholarly works by Bruce Metzger or F.F. Bruce are excellent. At a popular level, the material in Josh McDowell's *The New Evidence that Demands a Verdict* and Lee Strobel's *The Case for Christ* is very helpful (in that these latter two books are popularizing accounts of some of the leading work done by scholars like Metzger and Bruce).

While such details are indeed very important, I am bypassing them here. I mention them, however, because a solid case for the resurrection sometimes includes a defense of the trustworthiness of the biblical accounts. Since the primary witness to the resurrection is found in the pages of the Scriptures, the reliability of the Scriptures is an important plank in the case's foundation. In other words, the question is, "Do we have good reasons to trust the Bible's account of the resurrection?" And the answer, it would seem, on the basis of the normal historical investigation of the written sources, is yes. Certainly such considerations are not coercive (i.e., they do not force assent) for belief; but they certainly do not hurt. Perhaps their value is more limiting and negative—there is no historical reason to reject the claims of the Gospels on the basis of the normal criteria used to judge the trustworthiness of historical documents. (Hold on to the naturalistic causation objection: it will be dealt with—hopefully in a satisfactory manner—later in this chapter. But let it be said now that if historians can only appeal to naturalistic explanations—like scientism's practitioners—then of course historical data and the miraculous will be seen to be mutually incompatible.)

Well, back to the ordinary, run-of-the-mill case for the resurrection of Jesus Christ from the dead. The first requirement is Jesus' death, and his death by crucifixion is well attested. It is recorded in the Bible that Jesus was then buried in a tomb, and many different groups knew where his body was placed. His friends knew, since sympathizers had asked for the body, and some of the women he knew saw where they buried him. The Jews knew, because they had a vested interest in this matter, and they asked Pilate to set out a guard to secure the tomb. Pilate granted their request, and a group of Roman guards were placed at the tomb. Some of Jesus' followers, the Jewish leaders, and the Romans knew where Jesus was buried. This, as will be made evident, is quite important.

Fifty days later, the disciples all stand in Jerusalem, the very city where Jesus had been sentenced to death, and they boldly proclaim that Jesus is the Messiah. There had been other people who had claimed to be the Messiah, and when they died *all* of their followers stopped believing that their leader had really been the Messiah. Yet, here the followers of a crucified Messiah were proclaiming that he really was the Messiah—in fact, he wasn't dead at all! Yes, Jesus certainly had been dead, but God raised him to life.

The following observations are worth making: A) The disciples had fled in terror when Jesus was arrested. During his crucifixion, they stayed at a distance, and Peter even denied knowing Jesus at all. B) Fifty days later they were fully over their fear and loudly preaching *to the same people who killed Jesus* that Jesus was the Messiah of God. C) They knew that the enemies of Jesus could quite likely kill them for what they were saying, and they also knew that the enemies of Jesus knew where he had been buried.

Why are these three facts significant? First, a tremendous change had occurred in the lives of the disciples. They had gone from being cowards when they were with the person they thought was the Messiah to being brave when he was gone. If Jesus was still dead (i.e., if Jesus was a failed Messiah) why would the disciples be braver after his death and burial than when he was alive? Second, they knew that they could easily be put to death, or simply discredited by the authorities, if the authorities pointed out Jesus' tomb. Remember, the Jewish leaders knew where Jesus was buried. All they had to do to stop the disciples was to point the crowds down to the tomb. Even if the body was fairly decomposed, it would still bear the telltale signs of crucifixion.

One of the major facts in the case for the resurrection is that the tomb Jesus was buried in was, when the disciples preached at Pentecost, totally empty. If it was not empty, the Jewish leaders would have pointed out this rather inconvenient fact when Peter started talking about the resurrection of Jesus. A bodily resurrection with the dead body still in the tomb is a pretty weak message, and one which is easily discredited.

The Jewish leaders did not, of course, produce the body, or even point people to the tomb where Jesus was buried. This is because they had been circulating the story that the disciples had stolen the body of Jesus from the tomb. Interestingly enough, this is proof that the Jewish leaders were convinced the tomb was empty. They knew where the tomb was, they had asked for a guard, and they were saying that the body had disappeared because the disciples came along and stole it.

Perhaps the disciples did steal the body (after somehow getting past the Roman guard). The story ran that the guards had fallen asleep, since nobody would have believed this rag-tag group of fisherman overpowered trained Roman soldiers on guard duty. There was only one small difficulty with this story: Roman guards did not fall asleep on duty. Now, of course it wasn't that this *never ever* happened, but when they did fall asleep on guard duty they were put to death. This, needless to say, provided a powerful stimulant to combat fatigue. Roman soldiers were unbelievably disciplined and did not just nod off. The falling asleep story was a rather transparently concocted excuse to hide the truth of whatever it was that really happened.

Anyway, let it be assumed that the Roman soldiers really did fall asleep, and the disciples really did steal the body. Since the disciples have the body, and they know Jesus is dead, why would they go and preach that he was alive, risking death in the process? Perhaps they thought they could start a religious movement or profit from it tremendously in some nefarious way. If they thought they stood to gain from their lie, they were quickly brought back to reality. For their preaching they got beat up, insulted, and thrown in jail. Furthermore, they were threatened with death, and very early on Christians were being murdered for their faith. People will die for what they think is true, but people don't willingly suffer and die for what they know is false. If the disciples knew Jesus was dead, they would not have *all* suffered for it their whole lives, and then died in martyrdom. Surely that would be a greater miracle than the resurrection!

Something happened to convince the disciples that Jesus was raised from the dead. The empty tomb alone would have only caused confusion. No, it was only after Jesus appeared to his disciples that they were transformed from cowards into brave preachers and martyrs. Some have conjectured that the disciples experienced a mass hallucination, but this is extremely far-fetched. Everything known about hallucinations is against it. First, the doubting, cowardly disciples were not in a mindset conducive to such a phenomenon. Secondly, hallucinations are personal. Even if a crowd of sleep deprived people have hallucinations, the content is quite diverse. One person has a hallucination of pink flying elephants, while another has one of crawling bugs on a sandwich. There is no uniform content. Thirdly, even if the disciples had hallucinations of the risen Christ, the tomb would then not be empty. And if the tomb was not empty, the Jewish leaders at Pentecost would have taken the crowd down to the tomb where Christ's body lay.

While we are on the subject of far-fetched explanations, there is a really good example of the lengths some people will go to in order to provide a non-miraculous explanation of the empty tomb and appearances of Jesus to his followers. The Swoon Theory (which has been taken, very, very seriously by many, many people) states that Jesus did not die on the cross—he swooned. Then the Roman soldiers either mistakenly thought he was dead and buried him, or else they were in on the act and pretended to think he was dead (conspiracy theories abound!). Either way, Jesus was not really dead when he was buried. In the cool of the tomb he revived, then got up and walked out of the tomb, past the guards, and out into the wide world to convince his disciples that he was the risen Lord of Glory. So impressive was he that the disciples did not think he was the least bit troubled, and so they believed he was the resurrected Lord of all things. Jesus then left them (by walking up the mountain where he "ascended" by hiding), and either summarily died or withdrew to a distant land where he later died in obscurity—but not before, of course, he had married Mary Magdalene and had descendents who are clandestinely amongst us today. (Insert spooky music here for full effect.)

Well, the positives first. The Swoon Theory (and its variants) at least recognizes that the tomb was empty, and that the transformation of the disciples was owing to the fact that Jesus appeared to them after his "death." Since that about covers the positives, let's look at the negatives.

This theory is only instructive because it helps us to see the lengths people are willing to go to in order to exclude God from their reasoning. First, crucifixion tended to kill people, and the Roman soldiers knew what death looked like. If Jesus was not dead, he was so close they were fooled. Second, even if one survived being hung on a cross (and the flogging beforehand), it is obvious that such an ordeal would be extremely damaging to one's health. Tylenol and a good night's sleep do not remedy such an ailment. (As for those who say Jesus was a magician who started a drug cult, and he was revived after taking some herbs, *why* don't we use those herbs in medicine today if they're so effective they can "cure" someone from the trauma of a flogging and crucifixion? Please!) Third, the disciples did not react to Jesus by saying: "God preserved you from dying on the cross! Rome can't kill you!" They responded by believing that Jesus had truly died and truly come back to life. Not only so, but he was resurrected in a new and glorified body (not a crippled and damaged one which caused him to limp). Why would people believe the Swoon Theory? It would seem that people do not need more evidence as much as a new heart (although for some a new head couldn't really hurt either).

Many more fine details can be added to this general case for Christ's resurrection. For the present purpose, identifying two more will suffice. They are the conversion of the apostle Paul, and the theological spread of the doctrine of the resurrection. Paul—this is an incontrovertible historical fact—was converted from being a persecutor of the church to an apostle of Jesus Christ. According to Paul, it was because the Lord Jesus appeared to him. Paul was not primed to have a positive hallucination of Jesus. He hated Christians because they seemed to be advocating a failed Messiah and false worship. Paul did what he did with a clean conscious, believing he was serving God. Yet, Paul was appeared to by Jesus, and utterly transformed. This is another amazing post-crucifixion appearance which radically altered someone's life: and this one was to the sworn enemy of Christ, not to his followers. (James the brother of Jesus also fits into this category of conversion; but not as starkly.)

Doctrinally, the spread of the teaching of Jesus' resurrection is astounding in its original context. All of the first disciples of Jesus were Jews. Most Jews believed in the resurrection of the dead (but not all, like the Sadducees). For Jewish theology, the resurrection was something that would happen at the end of time, when the just would be raised in honor and the wicked raised in shame. The resurrection was an eschatological event for all people. Before Jesus *nobody thought in terms of a personal resurrection prior to this end-time event.* If Jesus was not resurrected—if the story was made up—it would never have spread very far, because the categories were all wrong. It would have been preposterous to tell Jews that somebody had been resurrected, because absolutely nobody thought of "resurrection" as being possible that way. If it was not the end of the age when all people were raised up it was just not the resurrection. A personal resurrection before the end was not in any one's mind as even a possibility, let alone an expectation.

How was it, then, that the early Christian message was that God's Messiah had died, and that he was resurrected (not merely revived or resuscitated)? Not only was this the message, but it was uniform in its growth. If the early church had simply made up stories about Jesus, there would undoubtedly have been some factions who denied Jesus' resurrection on theological grounds. Yet, as the church grew and the gospel spread, the good news was that Jesus had actually been resurrected. Perhaps those of us who are alive today are at such a conceptual distance from this Jewish understanding of the resurrection that we fail to see how shocking the idea of Jesus' personal resurrection would have been in the first century. Nevertheless, this brand new understanding of the resurrection to life was a central part of the Christian message right from the very beginning of the church. There will still be a general resurrection in the future, but in Jesus the firstfruits of this resurrection are already seen.

Jews would not have been readily converted to such an aberrant doctrine as the personal resurrection of Jesus in such a uniform manner unless it was based on truth. Furthermore, it was not only the Jews who were opposed to such a doctrine. Philosophically, the Greco-Roman culture surrounding the Jews thought that the idea of a bodily resurrection was utter nonsense. It was laughable. So Jesus' bodily resurrection would have been a new doctrine which was opposed by both Jew and Gentile….yet it uniformly flourished as the church grew and spread.

There are some who object at this point that the resurrection is a copycat doctrine borrowed from pagan mystery religions. Those who argue this way maintain that resurrec-

The Resurrection

tions were well attested in other religions, and that the Christians just stole the idea. This charge is—completely and utterly—false. Other religions had accounts of life-and-death cycles for their gods (e.g., a deity dies in the winter, comes to life in the spring). But these cycles happened year after year after year, and they could not be meaningfully called a bodily resurrection. In Egypt the god Osiris was said to be killed, but he came to life as the ruler of the shadowy underworld. He was cut up into more than a dozen pieces, and reassembled. Again, it is hard to see this as a resurrection, since living in the underworld was hardly equated with being fully alive. Another case—the supposed parallels with Mithras—are even less concrete. The written records of Mithras actually *postdate* Christianity, and there is no record of Mithras ever dying. As was mentioned at the beginning of this chapter, if you are going to have a resurrection you at least need to have a death!

Space forbids going into exhaustive detail about every possible objection to the historical fact of the resurrection. Some individuals argue—in essence—that miracles do not happen, so the resurrection did not happen. This argument is, on the face of it, rather thin. If miracles do not happen then they do not happen (as C.S. Lewis was quick to point out), but it is illegitimate to dismiss a reported miracle because such things allegedly simply do not happen. Such an approach severely begs the question.

Softening the objection, however, others argue that the probability of a given miracle happening is quite low, so suspending belief about a reported miracle, or even being skeptical about it is the rational stance to take. In regular life, this is certainly a fair position. But when there is good evidence for the validity of a reported event—even if it is hard to believe or very improbable—we are not at liberty to suspend belief. I know that it is grossly improbable for anyone to win the lottery, but if my friend wins I cannot doubt his good fortune on nothing more substantial than the basis that his winning was a very improbable event.

Furthermore, the likelihood of an event like the resurrection goes up dramatically if God exists. In fact, if God exists, there is no reason to doubt that miracles could and even would be part of his plan. If Jesus was God incarnate and died as a substitutionary atonement for sinners, such a unique event could very well anticipate an equally unique ending. Located in the Christian worldview, the resurrection is a perfectly understandable event. After all, it was not just a regular person dying a regular death—it was the Son of God dying for others.

One more common objection is that historians (much like scientists!) cannot ever appeal to a supernatural cause in their investigations of the past. Only natural explanations are permitted. So, the historian says there is an empty tomb, the disciples were transformed, a new theological understanding of the resurrection occurred, etc., but this is where it stops. The facts must be left uninterpreted, or at least interpreted apart from the supernatural. What can be said in response to this line of reasoning?

First, there is a sense in which it is true. Just like scientists, historians try to piece together data to fit into a material framework. There is nothing obscene about this practice, except when—as some scientists particularly go on to do—the claim is made that if it is not "natural" it is not knowable. Or, even worse, if science and historical study do not have the tools to discover the supernatural, then the conclusion is drawn that the supernatural cannot exist. The arrogance associated with this last claim is staggering, but it is what scientism is all about. At the least historians may not be able to appeal to a supernatural cause; but if that is the case they cannot deny the possibility of a supernatural cause either, especially if there is no good naturalistic theory which accounts for all of the data.

Second, the accidental details of history cannot *prove* the actions of a supernatural being. Apologists who think the historical case for the resurrection *proves* the existence of God are flatly wrong. The jump from historical facts (even when they are undeniable) to a supernatural explanation cannot be made with 100% certainty on the grounds of logical inferences alone. The evidential case is just that—a case based on evidence which is reasonable, but which falls short of absolute, incontrovertible proof. (Actually, this point isn't really debated too much—at least by scholars, evidentialists included.) I personally think the case is quite good (especially when made at great length, unlike here), but it is certainly not perfectly airtight. What historical case is?

This last question pushes us towards the great issue in Christian apologetics. It is the question of epistemology. How do we know things? How can we be certain that our knowledge is correct? Should we be skeptics? An accounting of epistemology is crucial in all areas of life. The next chapter will work through some of these issues.

Chapter Ten

EPISTEMOLOGY

Many people seem to think that Philosophy 101 involves sitting around discussing how we are to know that the chair in the corner of the room really exists. This caricature is very misleading. Such a discussion is far too advanced for the 101 level; it normally occurs in one's senior year or at graduate school! Even the question seems aggravating to many people. "How do I know the chair is real? Because I just know it. End of discussion."

Besides being an exercise in frustration, there is normally a point or two associated with this experiment. It gets people to think about what can be known, and how our beliefs can be justified. It raises issues about the reliability of our sense perceptions and our reasoning faculties. Furthermore, it makes us reflect on how we come into contact with the external world, and how we take many of our experiences for granted. It is easy to believe something (like the fact that the chair actually exists), but can I go a step further and offer a cogent reason for my acceptance of that belief?

Epistemology is the field of study that examines issues surrounding knowledge. What do I know? What can be known? How do we separate true from false beliefs? These types of questions are very important for apologetics. In the final analysis, the question, "What are the facts?" leads to a deeper question: "What *is* a fact?" This, in turn, moves from the objective to the subjective: "How do I know or recognize a fact?" Sometimes simple questions can demand very complicated answers. As a result, this chapter is likely to be the most oversimplified of the book. For those who are familiar with epistemology, it is hoped that you will be able to discern the deep structure below the surface structure. For those who have never thought about thinking before, it is hoped that this will be an accessible, easy, and reliable introduction.

Let us say that there are three boys. We will call them Michael, Mark, and Jordan. They all love hockey (especially Jordan who almost made the NHL), but they each cheer for different professional hockey teams. Much time is spent debating the merits and demerits of each club (these three boys debate about everything, incidentally). Michael has the misfortune of cheering for the Toronto Maple Leafs, who have not won the Stanley Cup in forty years. Given their current finish to the last season (missing the playoffs, again), and given their inefficiency at improving their roster in the off-season, it would seem statistically unlikely that the Leafs are going to win the Cup next year. In fact, not a single hockey expert thinks they have any chance whatsoever.

Mark and Jordan laugh at Michael's bold predictions and guarantees that his favorite team is going to win the Stanley Cup. Michael, however, continues to insist that he *knows* the Maple Leafs are going to emerge next season as the champions. As the season begins, the Leafs start out struggling. They hover just above the bottom teams in the standings. Then they get hot, and inexplicably put together a small winning streak. Still more amazingly, just before they play their different opponents, key players on the opposing teams get injured and cannot play. Always facing disabled hockey clubs, the Leafs manage to earn the eighth ranking in their conference and squeak into the playoffs. All of the pundits jokingly survey the scene, and talk about how incredibly lucky the Leafs were to go through such an improbable string of fortunate breaks, and to get into the playoffs, despite their lack of talent. Michael, unfazed, simply states that he *knew* they would make it this far all along—much to the chagrin of Mark, the Montreal fan.

During their first round playoff match, the Leafs lose their first three games by huge margins, and stand on the brink of elimination. Then, the other team comes down with food poisoning. It is so severe they cannot field a full team, and minor league players are called up. The Leafs are barely better than their minor league opponents, but since the food poisoning is so severe for the other team, and its effects linger for the rest of the series, the Leafs win round one. Michael just laughs—he *knew* the Leafs would win.

Now, suppose incredibly improbable scenarios like this happen during every round of the playoffs, and the Leafs— as bad as they are—end up winning the Stanley Cup. It turns out that Michael's preseason belief that the Leafs would win the Cup was true. But could we honestly say that he *knew* it? The same question could be asked of lottery winners. Against all odds some individual wins the lottery, and then they insist they *just knew* they had the winning ticket. Or think of the prospective mother who *knows* the baby is a girl while the prospective father happens to *know* that the baby is a boy. Clearly one of them will turn out to be right, and that individual will probably tell the other one that he or she "knew it all along." But did they really *know* the sex of the baby, or did they just happen to believe something that turned out to be true?

Philosophers distinguish between *true belief* and *knowledge*. Someone can have a true belief that is just a lucky guess. Or they can have a true belief (like Michael's belief that the Leafs will win the Cup) that is actually so improbable it would be irrational to hold with any conviction. Nevertheless, some people hold beliefs that are true which are based on guesswork, hunches, or just plain misinformation. Think of someone who reads their daily horoscope, and is convinced that they are going to have a financial windfall. Later that day, they receive a phone call from an attorney, who informs them that a distant uncle has passed away, leaving a significant sum of money for them in his will. All day long the person believed they were about to have a financial windfall *and* it turned out to be true, but for those of us who think daily horoscopes are nonsense, we would have a hard time saying the person really *knew* they were going to get lots of money that day, even if they confidently believed it and turned out to have been right.

What is the difference, then, between true belief and knowledge? Knowledge is basically true belief that is justified (i.e. justified true belief). In other words, in order to have knowledge, a person must first of all believe something. This something must also be true. For example, you can believe that the earth is flat, but you can't *know* that it is flat because it isn't. Finally, you must have a justification for holding your true belief. Holding a true belief because your horoscope said something or other is insufficient. Another way of expressing these things is to say that *knowledge* differs from mere *true belief* when the one holding a particular belief has a sufficient amount of *warrant* for their belief. Now, there is a wide range of difference between justification and warrant in technical discussions, but those would take us well beyond our purpose here.

If any of this seems mildly (majorly?) confusing, a sketch of Alvin Plantinga's model of warrant should help clarify the last few paragraphs. Okay, the quote about to be given may not clarify things very much at all, but after unpacking it, I think it will help tremendously. Plantinga writes:

> More fully, a belief has warrant just if it is produced by cognitive processes or faculties that are functioning properly, in a cognitive environment that is propitious for that exercise of cognitive powers, according to a design plan that is successfully aimed at the production of true belief.[5]

Following Plantinga, we can easily break this model down into its component parts.

First, the whole idea of warrant is connected to proper function. Something functions properly when it reliably does what it is supposed to do. Digestive systems function properly when they digest food and spread nutrients throughout the body. Cars function properly when humans can reliably use them for transportation. It is obvious that the car broken down on the side of the highway is not functioning properly!

Second, since we are concerned with knowledge rather than digestion or transportation, it is our cognitive faculties that must be functioning properly. Our thinking processes must reliably form true beliefs. They must not be subject to

---

[5] *Warranted Christian Belief* (Oxford: Oxford University Press, 2000), Xi.

dysfunction. Mental illnesses, trauma to the head, strokes, and other such things can result in cognitive dysfunction or damage to our faculties. Thus, someone who is mentally ill may have beliefs produced by their cognitive faculties, but since these faculties are dysfunctional, the beliefs produced are not warranted.

Third, the individual who has cognitive faculties that are functioning properly must be in an environment that is compatible with the way their faculties work. For example, our lungs function properly when they allow us to breathe. If we were to be held under water, our lungs would still be trying to do what they are supposed to do, but they are now submerged in an environment (water) where they cannot work. For our minds, if we were to be placed into a world where many, many images are holograms, we would not know what was real and what was not. Our cognitive faculties were not designed to function in an environment where we are surrounded by holograms.

Fourth, proper function requires a design plan. Cars are designed for transportation, so when they do not transport us, we say they are broken down. If cars were not designed for transportation, it would make no sense to speak of them as having "broken down" when they cannot be used for that purpose. Our cognitive faculties, then, must be designed for the reliable production of true belief. If that is not what they are designed for, it becomes impossible to say they are "broken down" or "malfunctioning" when they produce bizarre or false beliefs. There is a strong implication here for the coherence of naturalistic evolution which we will examine in a moment.

Fifth, the design plan must be *successfully* aimed at the production of *true belief*. The design plan must not be incompetent. It must be successful. The aim of the design plan must be the production of true belief. An unsuccessfully designed cognitive faculty aimed at producing true beliefs could fail to deliver and simply produce false beliefs. A cognitive faculty successfully designed to produce false beliefs would produce false beliefs. Either way, in order to have true beliefs instead of false beliefs, the cognitive faculty must be successfully designed to produce true belief.

This model seems fairly cogent (and this bare sketch can be rigorously expanded, as Plantinga does when he sets it forth). It is, however, devastating to naturalism. This is because naturalism *does not have a design plan*. Furthermore, in naturalistic evolution, all adaptations are aimed *at survival*; they are not aimed *at truth*. In short, evolution by natural selection never aims at truth: it aims at survival.

It is entirely possible, of course, that surviving may best be accomplished by the production of *false* beliefs. People who have cancer often believe that their odds of surviving are far better than they really are. How many of us believe in practice if not in theory that something terrible "just can't happen to me"? Such an attitude allows us to take risks, and in the world of nature and survival, even though such a belief is utterly false, it may be the risk takers who end up reproducing and surviving. Note that such people take risks precisely because they hold to a false belief, and this false belief aids them in surviving.

This one quick example can be multiplied indefinitely. Perhaps the real world is so dreadfully frightening that human beings could not survive if they knew the truth. It could just be that natural selection eliminated those who comprehended how dangerous the world is, and left those who couldn't handle the truth and turned to illusions. Over time, the survivors may very well come to live in a sort of fantasy land, where they survive by being blissfully ignorant of the way things really are. This does not mean that every belief they hold is completely false; but it does mean that they could never be sure which belief was genuinely true and which was not. In other words, they could hold to many true beliefs, but they could never be justified or warranted in holding them. At the end of the day if our cognitive faculties are adapted to survival, true beliefs may or may not be something they reliably produce. We simply could not know which belief was which: And this would mean we would be irrational to hold to the validity of any given belief, *including our belief in naturalistic evolution*. Cognitively speaking, it is irrational to be a naturalistic evolutionist. But if God designed our cognitive faculties to produce true belief, and he placed us in a good world where they can properly function, we have every reason to trust our reason. Christian thinking can be warranted; naturalistic thinking cannot.

Leaving aside Plantinga's model of knowledge as warranted true belief, there are other reasons for believing that human knowledge is only coherent if we are created by God. In what follows, I will be following some of the arguments of the presuppositionalists like Cornelius Van Til, Greg Bahnsen, and John Frame. One of their main contentions is that the idea of knowledge (epistemology) is inseparable from metaphysics (the way things really are). This means that knowledge only makes sense if certain conditions actually obtain. The precondition for knowledge, according to the presuppositionalists, is the existence of the Triune God.

There are several reasons for this position, and they will not all be examined here. One of the main arguments, however, is that only the existence of the Trinity resolves an old philosophical problem called "The One and the Many." Simply put, this problem is concerned with ultimate reality. What is *ultimate* in reality? Is it one thing, or is it many things? Is it a single undifferentiated monad, or is it a plurality of utterly unconnected things? If it is the former, then it cannot be divided in any way, and this means that it is impossible to observe differences at an ultimate level. Everything, ultimately, is just the same. If it is the latter, then it cannot be united in any way, and ultimately nothing can be compared or contrasted with anything else, since everything is totally dissimilar. Either way, *in an ultimate sense*, reality is incapable of being classified or meaningfully understood. Facts are either identical or so diverse they bear no relation to each other. Ultimately, then, which ever way one goes, knowledge is lost either in its ultimate identicalness or in its ultimate unrelatedness.

The God of the Bible, however, is revealed to be one God in three persons. In his oneness, God is a unity. In his threeness, God is diverse. Which is ultimate in the Godhead, the oneness or the threeness? Neither is ultimate at the expense of the other; they are *co-ultimate*. In the God Who Is, unity and diversity are eternally, infinitely, and ultimately contained. God, as self-contained ultimate reality, allows for both a unity which connects, and a plurality which allows for differentiation. Since ultimate reality is connected yet diverse, knowledge becomes possible.

Like Plantinga's model, presuppositionalists also argue that the human mind must be designed and functioning in a suitable environment for the production of true beliefs. Since the time of Kant many philosophers have noted the difference between our internal perceptions and the existence of the external world. How do I know that what's going on inside my head is actually meaningfully connected to what exists out there? Since all I have access to are my perceptions and internal thoughts, how is it meaningful or legitimate to apply my internal experiences to the external world (presuming such a world actually exists)? Well, on naturalism, there is no good reason to assume that what goes on inside my head meaningfully relates to the external world. But if human beings are created by God and placed in a good world (metaphysics), then we have reason to suppose that our internal thoughts and perceptions really do correspond in a meaningful way to the external world (epistemology). Remove God from the equation, and if you have a random universe and unguided mutation, you have no reason to think that your thinking is cogently connected to reality.

Another argument is that knowledge requires omniscience. Since facts stand in relationship to each other, unless the entire set of knowledge is comprehended, there is no way of knowing that you know any one thing truly. It may turn out that something you thought you knew you really didn't, because you were ignorant of another fact that overturned your previous belief. Human beings know *so very little*, it is quite possible that we don't actually know anything for sure, given naturalism. If God exists, however, he is omniscient. This means that God knows everything exhaustively because he knows how every single fact and possibility cohere. Since God is omniscient, *true, exhaustive, knowledge genuinely exists.* Since we are created by this omniscient being, he has designed our cognitive faculties to produce beliefs which align with his own. Thus, although we are not omniscient, since omniscience does exist, there is genuine, pure knowledge. At base, reality is rational and coherent. As such, we can have genuine knowledge, even though it is partial; our knowledge is grounded and assured as a subset of God's.

Why are so many philosophers skeptics? The reason is because they understand that, given naturalism, there is no reason for them to assume they actually know anything. In fact, there are reasons for them to doubt their beliefs. On a more popular level, many people are becoming selective relativists. Truth is relative to them (at least when it's convenient). Again, on the basis of naturalism, relativism and skepticism make good sense, *which is a huge problem!* The problem is that being a naturalist should make one see that reality and our thinking cannot be justified as rational. In other words, we have no good reason to suspect that our thinking is, at bottom, *rational.* But, if this is the case, if our thinking is *ir*-rational, why should we trust our conclusion that it is irrational? Wouldn't it be *rational* to think our thinking is irrational? And if our irrationalism relies on rationality, but rationality leads to irrationalism, we are stuck in a vicious, vicious circle. We are left as skeptics who do not even know that skepticism is true. We are rationally committed to irrationalism, or irrationally committed to rationalism. Whichever way we turn, it should be clear that no true belief we hold could be warranted or justified. And if this is the case, there is no such thing as knowledge. At best we hold true beliefs, but we do not really *know* anything at all.

What do these reflections have to do with the other apologetic arguments outlined in the previous chapters? Well, everything. If the Triune God of the Bible has not revealed himself to us, we cannot have knowledge. If we cannot have knowledge, we certainly cannot know that God does not exist. If we do claim to know anything, that claim itself depends entirely on the existence of the Triune Creator who made us in his image and successfully designed our cognitive faculties to produce true beliefs in the environment in which he placed us. If there is knowledge, there is God. If there is God, there is knowledge. *The very fact that the existence of God can be discussed demands his existence in order to be intelligible.* To deny God's existence depends on his existence—which is clearly a self-refuting position. Either way the atheist loses: to argue for the non-existence of God is to embrace a position that actually depends on God's existence, whereas to accept the existence of God is to cease to be an atheist! Knowledge is required for the debate, and God is required for knowledge. Our arguments do not prove the existence of God; but the very act of arguing about facts presupposes his existence. In the end, to deny the existence of God is to implicitly affirm that he is real!

Chapter Eleven

CONCLUSION

This book has attempted to provide a survey of some key elements in the gospel of Jesus Christ. The character of God, the nature of the fall into sin, and the perfect atonement provided by Jesus have all been briefly examined. Some of the numerous implications of the gospel's transforming impact have also been noted. Finally, some of the rational arguments and evidence for the existence of God have been canvassed. In the end the result is that, unless God exists, we cannot even intelligently argue about anything. Accepting the validity of human knowledge depends on the precondition of God's existence. To accept the former is to implicitly accept the latter. In other words, God's existence is a transcendental necessity for human knowledge.

God is to be praised, worshiped, and adored. He is utterly wonderful. Our rebellion against him is not only unacceptable, it is completely abhorrent. The just punishment for sin is death. In great grace, love, and mercy (not to mention holy justice), God plans and accomplishes the redemption of his people. They are purified from their sins, and the wrath of God's justice is fully satisfied by the substitutionary atonement of God incarnate, the Lord Jesus Christ. Not only are our sins taken away and their penalty paid by Jesus Christ, but his positive righteousness is imputed to our account. By faith, Jesus' righteousness is reckoned or credited to us as our very own.

Only the Triune God Who Is can fulfill our every righteous desire. He is the standard of goodness and beauty. He is the standard of rationality. Both intelligence and aesthetics are contained in him and flow from him. Sin has corrupted our faculties, and now we long for that which is wicked, and we try to find our own way to a fulfilling life. Every such effort is doomed to eternal failure. It is only in God that life is meaningful, and only in God that a transcendent being worthy of worship is found. Our alienation from God means death; our reconciliation to God through Jesus Christ brings eternal life.

Why must we save the saving gospel? There is *no other gospel that saves*. If we lose the biblical truths set forth in the Scriptures, there is no hope remaining. Salvation is of the Lord. It is by him and through him and for him. It is freely offered to all. In sovereign grace the power of the gospel goes forth to the ends of the world. As God works the lost are found, the blind see, the deaf hear, the lame leap for joy, and the prisoners are set free. For all of eternity we the redeemed will praise God and rejoice forever in his glorious presence, and we will only do so because of the saving gospel—the saving truth of what Jesus Christ has done for sinners like us.